Cucina Rapida

Cucina Rapida

quick Italian-style
home cooking

Clifford A. Wright

William Morrow and Company, Inc.

New York

For my mother,
Helen DeYeso Wright

Library of Congress Cataloging-in-Publication Data

Wright, Clifford A.
Cucina rapida : quick Italian-style home cooking / Clifford A.
Wright.
p.   cm.
Includes index.
ISBN 0-688-11532-2
1. Cookery, Italian.   2. Quick and easy cookery.   I. Title.
TX723.W75   1994   93-38079
641.5945—dc20   CIP

Printed in the United Sates of America

First Edition

1 2 3 4 5 6 7 8 9 10

BOOK DESIGN BY LINDA KOCUR

Acknowledgments

The joy of writing this book was in sharing food with family and friends and proving that it is possible to prepare delicious Italian-inspired dishes quickly.

I would especially like to thank Pam Haltom and Harry Irwin, David Forbes and Ginny Sherwood, and Eric Stange and Barbara Costa for their generous help in lending their kitchens, buying groceries, and offering opinions and for their friendship. Stephan Haggard and Nancy Gilson, Marsha Gordon, Christine Fairchild, Claudia Hautaniemi, and Faye Adams also lent kitchens and shared their opinions from time to time.

I tested several recipes while living in Venice, where I cooked for my Italian roommates, Francesca Piviotti and Giovanni Inghillieri. They flattered me by calling my *cucina rapida* authentic.

I also would like to thank my agent, Doe Coover, for her always extraordinary help and advice. My editor at William Morrow, Harriet Bell, whose suggestions kept me on the "fast" track, made this a better book. I am grateful for her patience and insight.

Clifford A. Wright
Arlington, Massachusetts

Contents

Introduction
1

one
The Cucina Rapida pantry
9

two
Pasta
23

three
Rice/Riso
75

four
Meat and poultry/Carne e pollame
83

five

Fish and shellfish/Pesce e frutti di mare

115

six

Frittatas and little sandwiches/Frittate e panini

139

seven

Vegetables and side dishes/Verdure e contorni

157

eight

Desserts/Dolce

183

Index

193

Introduction

I love to cook good food as much as I like to eat it. But although I enjoy spending a long Saturday afternoon in the kitchen preparing a special dinner for friends, my everyday cooking must be quick and uncomplicated. A busy schedule, three kids, and frequent guests mean I can't spend a lot of time in the kitchen. Yet while I need dinner on the table quickly, I refuse to sacrifice taste, quality, or freshness. Fast, fresh, and Italian-inspired food fits the bill.

When I lived in Italy, I discovered to my surprise that most Italians don't spend long hours in the kitchen. Today's Italians, like Americans, often need dinner on the table quickly. They also insist on preserving the quality of their cuisine. Where we eat prepared take-out food, Italians look for *cucina rapida,* quick Italian cooking.

Cucina Rapida provides recipes that go with today's lifestyle—quick for families on the go, light and healthy, made using ingredients that are often on hand, ideal for impromptu weeknight dinners, wonderful for leftovers, and popular with kids.

Most people who want dinner on the table quickly want it not in an hour, as some "rapid" cookbooks would have it, but in half that time. We also want our food to be delicious, simple to make, and nutritionally balanced. Italian food fills all these requirements and for this reason I shun food fads and stick with home cooking, *cucina casalinga.*

As you use *Cucina Rapida*, trying recipes, choosing favorites, discarding others, the "idea" behind this book will emerge. Then you will begin to extrapolate in your own cooking. My only suggestion is to trust your judgment and taste, especially your taste: Taste the food as you cook, don't worry, and have a good time.

Although most of these recipes take thirty minutes or less, you must make the effort to shop for the quality ingredients that make Italian food so distinctive and wonderful. This means getting to the supermarket, of course, but also taking a trip to an Italian market and finding a reliable fishmonger and greengrocer.

As far as the work goes, you still need to peel that onion or chop that tomato. After all, this is *cucina rapida*, not fast food. But *cucina rapida* does not mean you will be racing around the kitchen like a madcap cartoon character. Work quickly but deliberately, without interruption whenever possible. I happen to work fast, a vestige of restaurant experience years ago, but I've taken this into account in the recipes. I have not factored in the time it will take you to read the recipe, clean pots, clear the table, or answer the phone.

The roots to my *cucina rapida* can be traced to several sources. My maternal grandfather was Italian, from the Campania region, and as a child I relished my mother's lasagne and baked rigatoni. Then in the late 1960s and early 1970s, I worked in Italian restaurants, where I refined my tastes.

I have long had a love of Italian food, born from my childhood but enhanced by many journeys to Italy. Once I began finding in my local supermarket products essential to good Italian cooking, such as a wide variety of very fresh vegetables, I realized that *cucina rapida* was a natural.

Cucina Rapida is not merely about cooking flavorful and fresh Italian-inspired food fast. It's about having your pantry and refrigerator stocked with all those wonderful ingredients that make the food glorious. (Chapter One tells you more about how to stock your pantry.)

Cucina Rapida relies on a well-stocked pantry and serendipitous leftovers. Have three slices of cooked bacon that no one ate at Sunday morning breakfast? Save it for Fusilli with Vegetables and Herbs (page 42). Leftover grilled fish from last night's barbecue? Try Grilled Bluefish, Penne, and Green Bean Salad (page 56).

The recipes in this book require several basic cooking techniques, which are outlined below.

sautéing

The most frequently used cooking method in *cucina rapida* is sautéing. To *sauté* (literally, "to leap") means to cook quickly, to toss in a small amount of fat in a pan over high heat. In most areas of Italy, the cooking fat of choice is olive oil. Olive oil imparts a light, fruity flavor to food and it is high in monounsaturates and more healthful than animal fats. In sautéing, a small amount of oil goes a long way. Use the amount called for in the recipe, and if you find food sticking, add a few tablespoons of water instead of more oil.

grilling

I use my gas grill or outdoor brick fireplace almost every summer day, and on many days throughout the Boston winter. The ease and convenience of a gas grill can't be beat—especially as it requires only ten minutes of preheating. Unfortunately, a gas grill never gets as hot as I would like, as with the heat of a charcoal or hardwood fire. A charcoal fire, on the other hand, takes thirty-five to forty-five minutes for the coals to become red hot. However, I consider that a painless amount of time, because once you light the charcoal the grill takes care of itself.

If you use a charcoal grill, I recommend the lightable charcoal briquette bags, found in supermarkets and wherever barbecue supplies are sold. To use, you place the bag in the well of the grill, under the grilling grate, then light the ends of the bag itself—no fuss with starters, newspaper roll-ups, pyramiding, or lighter fluid.

If you use ordinary charcoal briquettes, form them into a pyramid about twelve inches in diameter at the base. A cylindrical metal can used for pyramiding charcoal, sold at barbecue supply stores, is handy. Liberally douse the briquettes with charcoal lighter fluid (if not presoaked) and set aflame at four separate points. Once the flame dies out, in a few minutes, the coals have started to burn: There is no need to squirt more lighter fluid on them. The coals are ready when all are white with ash. Knock the ash off and begin grilling.

(If you don't have a grill, you can use your oven broiler.)

deep-frying

I find it curious that so many people won't deep-fry at home but think nothing of ordering fried zucchini at an Italian restaurant. Many people shy away from deep-frying because of the rightful concern about adding unnecessary fat to their diets. But properly fried food uses less oil than is found in most salad dressings.

Nevertheless, olive oil, as relatively healthful a cooking fat as it is, is still a fat. I love deep-fried foods, but I eat them only twice a month at the very most.

The secret to successful deep-frying is using fresh hot oil and keeping it consistently hot. Soggy, greasy fried food is a result of crowding too much food into the deep fryer and thereby lowering the temperature of the oil. If the temperature of the oil is lowered, the sealing effect is lost and oil soaks into the food you are trying to make crisp.

The temperature of the oil must stay regulated, usually between 350°F and 375°F, to assure crisp, well-fried food. If you have neither a deep fryer with regulated heat controls nor a candy thermometer to measure temperature, keep in mind that in a pot about 8 inches in diameter, 6 cups of oil (a depth of about 2 inches) will take 10 minutes of preheating over high heat before it is ready for deep-frying. I keep such a pot, an inexpensive one, solely for deep-frying in tandem with my deep fryer. I use one for olive-oil frying and one for vegetable-oil frying.

Deep-fried food must always be drained before serving to allow excess oil to drip off. Further draining on absorbent paper towels is also wise. You can save and strain relatively clean deep-frying oil, using paper oil strainers available in kitchenware stores and from deep fryer manufacturers. But it is best to replace the oil after the fourth or fifth use.

To dredge, or coat, foods for deep-frying, lay out a large piece of waxed paper, a dinner plate, and a cookie sheet or pan. Spread the specified amount of flour on one half of the waxed paper and the bread crumbs on the other half. Break the egg onto the dinner plate and lightly beat it. Dredge the food in the flour and shake or pat off the excess, dip it into the egg, and then dredge it in the bread crumbs. Then let the food rest on the cookie sheet in the refrigerator until you are ready to cook.

A simple method of dredging small amounts of food is to use two paper bags: Put the flour in one bag and the bread crumbs in the other. Place the food in the flour bag and shake to coat. Remove and dip the food in the beaten egg. Then place in the bread-crumb bag and shake to coat. Place on a cookie sheet until you are ready to cook. Just before deep-frying, shake or pat off excess coating. (Do not fry too many pieces of food at once.)

If you do a lot of deep-frying, consider investing in a deep fryer. It's worth it: Today's models are safe, convenient, and inexpensive.

boiling

While boiling water is the easiest cooking method in the world, there's a right and wrong way to do it. See page 17 for the proper method of cooking pasta.

microwaving

None of these recipes relies on a microwave. A microwave is a useful but not essential kitchen tool. I have a microwave, but I use it only for limited chores, such as reheating and defrosting.

food processors

I use my food processor for grinding nuts, for example, or pureeing, but rarely for chopping and slicing. When you add up the time it takes to pull it out, assemble it, and then wash all the parts, I find it's too much trouble. Nothing beats a couple of sharp knives.

Equipment

■ Soak pots and pans in hot water as soon as you finish with them to make cleanup easier.

■ Clean up as you work. Wash the pots you are not using while other food cooks, so you do not end up with a sink full of dirty pans.

■ Consider purchasing a spaghetti pot with colander and steamer inserts so you can cook spaghetti and steam vegetables at the same time.

■ When thinking of using "labor-saving" devices such as food processors or electric mixers, remember to factor in the time it takes to assemble, disassemble, and clean these gadgets or machines.

■ Keep a strainer handy for rinsing herbs and straining or draining ingredients.

Read the Recipe

■ Before you start cooking, read each recipe through at least two times, envisioning what happens when.

■ Remember that a long list of ingredients does not necessarily mean a long preparation or cooking time. Usually it's a matter of adding the ingredients to a sauce or putting them into a pan one after the other or all at once.

■ Have all the ingredients chopped, peeled, diced, and ready to go before you start cooking.

■ As you read a recipe, see what you can chop or mince together. In Penne with Yellow Pepper, Black Olives, and Tomatoes (page 33), for example, the onion, yellow pepper, and garlic can be chopped together.

■ Check to see if you can cook two items at once, for example, penne and green beans (see page 56).

■ When concocting menus, if you decide to make a more involved main course, be sure to pair it with simple side dishes, such as steamed vegetables.

Timesaving Techniques

- Put a large covered pot of water on to boil as soon as you walk in the house for pasta or vegetables.
- Chop onions by making a criss-cross pattern with a sharp knife and then slice horizontally.
- Pit olives quickly by lining them up and crushing with the flat side of a large knife.
- Peel garlic quickly by first crushing the clove lightly with the flat side of a knife to loosen the skin.
- Put anyone standing near you, including children, to work. For example, children love to "squeeze" food, so let them help with Croquettes of Veal with Apple, Walnuts, and Taleggio (page 94), Fried Meatballs (page 85), Meatballs Stuffed with Almonds, Mint, and Mozzarella (page 84), Sage Meatballs with Marsala Sauce (page 86), or Meatloaf Stuffed with Eggs (page 87).
- Learn to eyeball measurements. Put a tablespoon of grated cheese in the palm of your hand to see what it looks and feels like. Pour a tablespoon of oil into a pan and watch how it spreads, so that next time you can pour without a measure.
- Find a top-quality fishmonger—one whose fish always tastes fresh; who sells an interesting variety of fish, not only the most common species; and who sells shucked oysters, cooked lobster meat, cleaned squid, and shelled and picked cooked crabmeat.
- If you substitute cooked shrimp for unpeeled and uncooked shrimp in a recipe, remember that it will need only a minute of reheating.
- When buying poultry and meats, ask the butcher to bone or butterfly your selection, saving you time at home.
- When using fresh tomatoes in sauces, there's no need to peel and seed them if you are willing to accept a little more acidity and a few bits of tomato skin here and there in the sauce.
- Never throw away leftover bread—fresh or stale. It has uses besides bread crumbs—for example, in Fried Meatballs (page 85).

One

the

Cucina Rapida

pantry

Good food is simply good ingredients prepared well. People often ask me for recipes and, since I don't believe in "secret recipes," I gladly pass them along. There is a "secret" to good food, but it's not the recipe—it's the ingredients. No matter how precisely a recipe is written, it will not turn out well if you don't buy fresh, top-quality ingredients.

While most of the ingredients needed for cooking Italian food are readily available in supermarkets, sometimes the products sold in Italian groceries are of better quality, such as prosciutto di Parma, pancetta, whole anchovies, cheeses, and a wide variety of imported pasta.

Middle Eastern markets and Greek markets are good sources for certain bulk items used in Italian cooking that are more expensive in supermarkets or gourmet shops—for example, pine nuts or olive oil.

The recipes in this book are part of *cucina rapida*. But don't try to save time cooking only to add that time to the shopping. Keep your pantry well stocked with nonperishables from a one-time shopping trip and limit your daily shopping. My everyday shopping is usually only for bread and fresh vegetables.

Anchovies: Salted anchovies are an essential ingredient in Italian cooking. I use anchovies often, especially in sauces. To omit them when called for just because you don't like them on a pizza is to lose a unique and important seasoning. That is the key word—*seasoning:* Anchovies season sauces. Even my guests who say they dislike anchovies swoon over Fettucine with Anchovy Butter (page 27). But in the end, if you just don't like them, just don't use them.

I prefer the imported salted whole anchovies from Sicily sold in one-and-a-half-pound cans in Italian markets. Supermarkets sell filleted anchovies packed in oil in small cans.

Artichokes: Although fresh artichokes are superior, canned whole artichoke hearts packed in water or frozen artichoke hearts are an excellent substitute. Drain canned artichokes before using. Good-quality marinated artichoke hearts can also be found in supermarkets and Italian markets.

Bread: Look for freshly baked Italian bread with a thick, crunchy crust and a porous but chewy center. A crusty French baguette is a fine substitute.

Garlic bread, or bruschetta, is a good accompaniment to most Italian meals, or you can serve it while dinner is being prepared. Garlic bread is best made with fresh ingredients at the last moment. Here's a quick recipe:

garlic bread

6 thick slices Italian or
    French bread

½ cup olive oil

3 garlic cloves, peeled and
    very finely chopped

5 tablespoons finely
    chopped fresh parsley

Pinch of red chili pepper
    flakes

Preheat the oven to 400°F. Lay the slices of bread on a baking sheet. Mix the olive oil, garlic, parsley, and red pepper flakes. Evenly spoon the mixture over each slice. Toast in the oven for 4 to 8 minutes, depending on how crisp you like it. Serve.

Bread Crumbs: Make fresh bread crumbs in the food processor, using leftover day-old Italian or French bread. Store in the freezer, refrigerator, or kitchen cabinet. Italian markets sell fresh bread crumbs in plastic bags. Don't buy the tasteless bread crumbs sold in cans.

Butter: The recipes in this book use only unsalted butter.

Capers: Italian markets sell capers preserved in brine or salt in bulk from large barrels. These large capers are significantly cheaper than the small nonpareil capers sold in tiny jars. Stored in a tightly covered container, they will keep for between six months and a year.

Cheese: Artisanal cheesemakers around the country produce fresh mozzarella, ricotta, and mascarpone. Look for these products in local Italian markets. Larger cheese manufacturers are also producing fresh cheeses now and one finds them, increasingly, in supermarkets. Fresh buffalo mozzarella is imported from Italy, but it is very expensive.

When buying fresh cheeses, such as mozzarella, buy only as much as you are likely to use within two days. For table cheeses such as Bel Paese or Taleggio, buy as much as you are likely to use in one or two weeks. For grating cheeses, buy as much as you are likely to use in a month. Keep all of these cheeses well wrapped in plastic in the refrigerator.

Bel Paese: A mild, creamy cheese. It is a good table or dessert cheese. Serve at room temperature.

Caciocavallo: A hard cow's milk cheese, usually formed into the shape of a gourd and sold in pairs tied to each other. Caciocavallo is a grating cheese that becomes sharper with aging. If unavailable, substitute an imported provolone. Store Caciocavallo whole; do not grate until needed.

Fontina: A cheese from the Piedmont, this is made from whole cow's milk in the summer but often from sheep's milk during other seasons. When you buy imported Italian Fontina, look for cheese from the Val d'Aosta. It has a thin brown rind enclosing a soft pale cheese with tiny holes. Fontina Val d'Aosta is creamier, more flavorful, and more expensive than Fontina Valbella, which has a brownish-purple outside. Fontina is used in cooking, as it melts very well, and as a table cheese. Serve at room temperature. I do not recommend Danish or Swedish Fontina.

Gorgonzola: Gorgonzola, made from whole cow's milk, is a blue cheese with a high fat content. Taste before buying: It should be rich and creamy with a sharp flavor but never bitter. Serve at room temperature.

Mascarpone: This rich cheese looks like clotted cream. It has a very high fat content and is curdled with citric acid. It is available packaged in plastic tubs and fresh. Mascarpone is sometimes layered with other cheeses, such as Gorgonzola, or with herbs and nuts. Use within three days.

Mozzarella: Today most mozzarella in the United States and Italy is made from cow's milk, but originally it was made only from water buffalo milk. There is still some mozzarella produced in Italy from water buffalo milk. Fresh mozzarella should be milky white and dripping in its whey juices. Packaged commercially produced mozzarella is neither moist nor flavorful. Store fresh mozzarella in a bowl of water in the refrigerator, changing the water once a day. It will keep for three days.

Parmigiano-Reggiano (Parmesan): Grated Parmesan is irrevocably linked with pasta and tomato sauce in most American households, but when cut fresh from a large wheel of cheese, Parmigiano-Reggiano is also a good eating cheese. Buy imported Parmigiano-Reggiano; the rind will be stamped with its name.

Don't grate Parmesan until you need it, or it will dry out and lose its flavor. Avoid the tasteless grated Parmesan sold in supermarkets. Pass a chunk of Parmesan at the table with a hand-held grater so diners can grate the cheese themselves.

Pecorino: A hard sheep's milk cheese used for grating. Don't grate Pecorino until you need it, or it will dry out and lose its flavor. Pecorino Pepato is a Sicilian variation of Pecorino, with black peppercorns mixed into the curd.

Provolone: A hard cow's milk cheese usually formed into a giant sausage shape. It is similar in taste to Caciocavallo. When you buy provolone for cooking purposes, make sure you buy the mild imported version.

Ricotta: Italian markets often sell freshly made ricotta. Fresh ricotta will keep in the refrigerator for about four days. Supermarkets sell ricotta in containers, including a low-fat type, that is fine for cooking.

Ricotta Salata: Although this term can refer to a Pecorino, the type you will find in the market is a dried ricotta. The fresh cheese is placed in a perforated container and pressed, then left to dry in a special curing room. There are two varieties of ricotta salata, one for eating and a harder one for grating.

Taleggio: A semisoft whole cow's milk cheese from Lombardy, pale yellow and mild-tasting, with a thin rind. It is a good table cheese, also used in cooking because it melts well. Serve at room temperature.

Cream: Heavy, or whipping, cream is used in some of these recipes. Recipes with butter and cream are common in northern Italy and in French-influenced Italian *alta cucina.*

Currants: Packaged dried California currants are available in supermarkets. I often use currants or raisins in dishes that have Sicilian origins, such as Baked Stuffed Zucchini (page 180).

Fish: Today's fishmongers offer a variety of filleted fish, making our lives easier. Unfortunately, it's harder to judge the quality of fillets than of whole fish, whose freshness can be tested using touch, smell, and sight. And a soaking in sodium benzoate can disguise a poor-quality fish fillet.

There is only one sure way to determine the freshness of filleted fish, and that is through taste. Therefore, the best guide is to try fish from a variety of markets until you find a store where the fish is consistently good. Fresh fish should not taste "fishy," nor should the store smell "fishy"—it should smell like the briny ocean.

Top-quality fishmongers can often be found in ethnic neighborhoods where fish cookery is important to the culture, such as Japanese, Chinese, Vietnamese, Italian, Greek, Portuguese, or Caribbean enclaves. Top-quality fish will taste good unadorned, while lesser-quality fish will taste insipid and generic no matter how you prepare it. Choose the freshest fish, then choose the recipe.

Garlic: Store garlic in a cool dry place; it does not need refrigeration. Garlic has a pungent flavor, and adding more garlic to a recipe does not make the dish "more" Italian. In some recipes, I flavor my cooking oil by sautéing crushed raw garlic in the oil and then discarding it. Cooking the garlic only while the oil heats ensures that the garlic won't burn and give off an acrid smell or bitter taste. Remove the garlic as soon as it begins to color.

Herbs and Spices: Italian cooking uses herbs and spices to a great degree and with much variety. Fresh parsley and basil and fresh and dried oregano are the most important herbs in Italian cuisine. Since they are so perishable, do not wash the leaves of fresh herbs until you are ready to use them. When a recipe calls for a fresh herb that you don't have, it is often better to leave it out or replace it with fresh parsley rather than using the dried herb.

Basil: Do not attempt to replace fresh basil with dried, which has an entirely different flavor.

Bay Leaves: Bay leaves sold in bulk in Italian or Middle Eastern markets are less expensive than those in the supermarket spice rack. They are used frequently for separating and flavoring pieces of meat on skewers when grilling or for flavoring broths.

Black Pepper: These recipes assume freshly ground black pepper.

Fennel Seed: These licorice-flavored seeds keep well.

Marjoram: This is a subtle herb, best fresh, stronger when dried.

Mint: Fresh mint is an essential herb in many recipes. Do not replace it with dried mint, which is much too intense for recipes calling for fresh mint.

Oregano: Oregano, both fresh and dried, is a cornerstone of Italian cooking.

Parsley: I use flat-leaf Italian parsley, although curly leaf is fine. Dried parsley has no taste; do not use it.

Peppercorns: I keep whole black and white peppercorns on hand for freshly ground pepper when needed. Green peppercorns usually are sold in brine in small cans and should be stored in the refrigerator after opening.

Rosemary: A strong flavorful herb that is good dried, even better fresh; a single sprig can go a long way.

Saffron: A powerful, and expensive, spice used in minuscule proportions. Spanish saffron, the most common, is available as threads or powder. The threads are more versatile and go further. Saffron should be bright orange-red in color, not crimson. Store in a tightly sealed container in a dark place.

Sage: If you do not have fresh sage, omit it rather than substituting dried sage, which is just too musty-tasting for Italian food.

Salt: These recipes use common table salt, although you may prefer coarser sea salt or kosher salt when cooking seafood.

Savory: Dried savory is used in these recipes.

Thyme: Most of these recipes use fresh thyme, but dried thyme usually is fine.

Honey: Any honey will do, but I like the subtlety of orange blossom honey.

Liqueur: For cooking purposes, I keep small "airplane" size miniatures of liqueurs such as brandy, Frangelico, peach schnapps, and kirsch on hand.

Mushrooms: A number of these recipes call for exotic mushrooms, such as portobello, cremini, and shiitake. I can find these mushrooms in my supermarket now, but if you cannot, substitute common, button, or field mushrooms. Dried mushrooms are not used in *cucina rapida* because they require too much soaking time.

Nuts: Nuts can quickly turn rancid. Store in tightly sealed jars in the refrigerator, or freeze them.

Almonds: Buy whole blanched almonds; whole nuts keep best. Several of these recipes call for roasted ground almonds. To prepare them ahead of time, preheat the oven to 425°F. Spread the almonds in a single layer on a baking sheet and place in the oven until they turn light brown. Let cool, grind them in a food processor, and store in a jar in the refrigerator until needed.

Hazelnuts: Buy whole hazelnuts, sold less expensively in bulk in Italian and Middle Eastern markets.

Pine Nuts: Called *pignoli* or *pinoli* in Italian, pine nuts are far less expensive in Italian and Middle Eastern markets than in supermarkets or specialty shops.

Pistachios: Buy pistachios both shelled and whole. When crushed they should have a pretty bright green color. I find bulk pistachios in Middle Eastern markets to be both cheaper and of better quality than supermarket pistachios. Never use red-dyed pistachios for cooking (or eating, for that matter).

Sesame Seeds: Roast before using.

Walnuts: The supermarket variety is fine.

Olive Oil: The best olive oil is extra virgin oil. The range of prices for extra virgin can be great: I have seen a quart of Tuscan extra virgin olive oil selling for $32 next to a gallon of Greek extra virgin selling for $24. Your best bet, if you're on a budget, is to look for high-quality but less popular extra virgin oils from Italy's southern regions, such as Apulia and Sicily. Spanish, Greek, and Lebanese olive oils are less expensive but also less widely available.

I recommend keeping two or three different grades of olive oil on hand. I use a lower-grade "pure" oil for deep-frying, a "virgin" or inexpensive "extra virgin" olive oil for sautéing, and a high-quality extra virgin for table use. If you use a lot of olive oil, buy it in gallon cans, which will be cheaper than buying it in 8- or 16-ounce bottles. Although olive oil can become rancid when exposed to air and sun, a can—rather than a bottle—of oil stored in a dark cool place can keep for a year. (But if you are cooking every day, it will be used long before that time.)

I like to use homemade infused olive oils for cooking. Putting garlic, herbs, or chili peppers in olive oil to steep infuses the oil with their flavor. One of my favorites is red pepper oil: Buy a 1-pint can of olive oil and put twenty whole dried red chili peppers into it. The flavor is best after the oil has steeped for at least one week, when you can use it on pasta or for dipping bread.

Olives: Taste olives whenever possible before buying them so you know what you are getting. There is an enormous variety of olives from many regions and countries, with a variety of tastes.

The names of various olives reflect a type or the region where they are grown—for example, Niçoise, Kalamata, Gaeta, Paternò, Calabrese, and so on. Sicily, Morocco, and Greece all produce tangy cured black olives that have a unique taste. I find canned olives from California devoid of flavor.

If you buy olives from the barrel at Italian or Middle Eastern markets, make sure your container has some of the liquid in which they were stored.

Pancetta: Pancetta, sometimes called Italian bacon, is cured but not smoked. If you are unable to find pancetta, replace it with bacon blanched for a couple of minutes in boiling water.

Pasta: Pasta is at the center of *cucina rapida.* Although fresh pasta takes only a few minutes to cook, it does not hold up to the greater variety of sauces and additions that dried pasta can manage. Therefore, I use only dried pasta in this book because most of my pasta recipes are hearty and work better with dried pasta.

Follow the directions on the package for dried pasta. Pasta should be cooked in abundantly salted (about 3 to 4 tablespoons), furiously boiling water, a minimum of 6 quarts for a pound of pasta. Add the pasta gradually to the water so it doesn't stop boiling, then reduce the heat to medium high and cook until done.

When the pasta is done, it should be *al dente,* literally, "to the teeth"—not soft, not hard, but with a little "bite" to it. Drain the pasta in a colander and shake the excess water out (unless the recipe specifies otherwise). Do not run cold water over the pasta—it only washes away nutrients.

While it is interesting to have a wide variety of dried pastas on hand, you can make do with the basics: spaghetti, fettucine, and macaroni or penne.

Many excellent, often locally produced, stuffed fresh pastas also are now available.

Be sure to save all the broken pieces of pasta remaining in the bottom of the box or package. When you have enough, make Pizzaiola Sauce for Leftover Macaroni (page 29).

The usual first-course serving of pasta in Italy is about four ounces of uncooked pasta. My recipes are based on this amount because I assume you will be serving the pasta along with something else. The whole point to *Cucina Rapida* is to avoid the work involved with serving a series of courses. But if you are serving courses, a pound of pasta will serve from four to six with a substantial meat, fish, or vegetable sauce. If you make the pasta recipes to serve as an entrée without other dishes, figure on six ounces per person, without sauce.

Peas: Fresh peas are exquisite in season. Frozen peas are vastly preferable to canned peas.

Peperoncini: Also called Italian long peppers or frying peppers, these mild long pale green peppers are available in most supermarkets. The word *peperoncini* also refers to hot chili peppers.

Porchetta: *Porchetta* is Italian roast pork, sold as a cold cut in Italian groceries. Ask for it by name or substitute any supermarket deli sliced roast pork.

Prosciutto: *Prosciutto* means ham. In Italy, one must specify *prosciutto cotto,* cooked ham, or *prosciutto crudo,* cured ham, which is what Americans mean by prosciutto. When you purchase prosciutto, make sure it is sliced thin enough to be translucent, unless you will be chopping it.

The best prosciutto crudo is prosciutto di Parma. I usually call for prosciutto di Parma when it is to be eaten raw. If the expense of prosciutto di Parma is prohibitive, or if you will be cooking the prosciutto, try the less expensive but very fine prosciutto made in North America.

Raisins: The golden California raisins known as "sultanas" are excellent, as are the black raisins sold as Zante raisins.

Red Bell Peppers: There are excellent roasted and peeled red peppers sold in jars. Roasted peppers are also available in bulk at Italian markets.

You can roast bell peppers yourself by holding each pepper over a burner until it blisters and turns black all over or by roasting the peppers in a 425°F oven until they blister and char. Once they are cool enough to handle, peel and seed them.

Red Chili Peppers: I prefer whole dried red chili peppers to flakes because they stay fresh longer, but for convenience and speed some of the recipes in this book call for flakes. One whole dried red chili pepper equals about ¼ teaspoon flakes.

Rice: Arborio rice, a short-grain rice, is the preferred rice in Italian cooking. Short-grain rice is essential for the dish known as risotto. (For more on risotto, see page 75.) Italian markets and many supermarkets sell Arborio rice.

Sardines: Maine sardines, or any sardines canned in water, are best for the recipes in this book that call for canned sardines. They are available in supermarkets. Canned sardines can never replace fresh when called for.

Sausage: The fresh sausages sold in Italian markets are usually fresher and more authentic than those found in supermarkets.

Soffritto: The word *soffritto* comes from the term *sotto friggere,* to under-fry or sauté gently. *Soffritto* is used to refer to both this method of sautéing and the mixture that is sautéed. A soffritto is a mélange of very finely chopped vegetables and herbs lightly sautéed in olive oil. Typically a soffritto consists of onions, celery, garlic, and parsley. It may also include any combination of these and other vegetables, such as carrots, herbs such as oregano, and cooking fats such as pancetta, lard, seed oil, or butter. A soffritto is usually the starting point of a more complex sauce or stew. Many of the pasta sauces in this book begin with a soffritto.

Squid: Most fishmongers now sell cleaned squid, a big time-saver. Squid follows the "4 and 40" rule: For perfect squid, you must cook it either for 4 minutes or for 40. Much more than 4 minutes of cooking will turn it tough and rubbery so you will need to cook it at least 40 minutes to have it become tender again. (For *cucina rapida*, you obviously cook it for just 4 minutes.)

Stock: For convenience and speed, canned stock or bouillon cubes are ideal for the recipes in this book that call for stock. I usually use bouillon cubes dissolved in hot water. There are low-sodium varieties of both canned stock and bouillon cubes available for those who wish to limit their salt intake.

Tomatoes: When fresh vine-ripened tomatoes are either unavailable or lacking in taste, substitute imported Italian canned plum tomatoes, purees, pastes, and sauces in any recipe.

The best canned whole plum tomatoes say "San Marzano" on the label. When shopping for tomato sauces, buy plain tomato sauce. (The imported sauces will say "salsa di pomodoro" on the label.) When buying tomato paste, look for the imported tubes of Italian tomato concentrate. They are of excellent quality and very convenient when you want only a tablespoon or so of tomato paste.

When shopping for fresh tomatoes, look for bright red tomatoes that are ripe but still slightly firm. Removing the seeds will reduce the amount of acidity, but it is OK to have some seeds; you don't have to get out every last one.

If you don't mind tomato skins, you don't need to peel them. If you prefer to peel fresh tomatoes, drop them into boiling water for about 30 seconds to a minute, remove, and pinch the skin off. Do not store ripe tomatoes in the refrigerator or their flavor will be diminished.

Tuna: Any brand of canned tuna is fine. Imported Italian canned tuna is usually packed in oil.

Vinegar: A quart each of red wine vinegar, white wine vinegar, and balsamic vinegar should last you a year or more.

Wine: Use good wine for cooking, often the same variety of wine you will drink with the dish. I cook a lot with wine and so keep good but not expensive wine on hand. For cooking, stock a dry white wine and a fuller-bodied red wine such as a Chianti. Some dishes use Marsala, a fortified wine from Sicily, which may be either sweet or dry.

a note on the recipes

Many of these recipes can be increased proportionally and served on their own as one-course meals. Read the paragraph on page 139 about increasing the yield of egg dishes.

If you have a grill, please read the information on page 3 before proceeding with the recipes. If you do not own a grill, you will have to set your broiler for recipes calling for grilling. Because broilers have differing temperatures, keep your eye on the food as it cooks.

There are several recipes that require some kitchen skills, such as peeling shrimp or shucking oysters, which might mean longer preparation times unless you find already shucked oysters and peeled shrimp.

Measurements for herbs should be considered as guidelines and need not be followed exactly.

Two

Pasta

Pasta dishes are the heart of *cucina rapida.* I could eat pasta every day. Cooking pasta is easy if you follow the basic guidelines on page 17. While the water reaches a boil and the pasta cooks, you can quickly prepare a sauce.

These pasta recipes will yield ample first-course portions, or serve them along with meat, fish, and vegetables, in which case they will provide generous servings.

For *cucina rapida* it is quickest and easiest to think of these pasta recipes as *piatti unici,* all-in-one dishes, rather than the traditional Italian first course, *primo piatto.* The rule of thumb, however, is four ounces dry pasta if you do serve it as a first course, six to eight ounces for a main course.

spaghetti with olive oil, parsley, and red chili pepper

1 pound spaghetti

3 tablespoons finely chopped fresh parsley

¼ cup extra virgin olive oil

1 dried red chili pepper, crumbled, or ¼ teaspoon red pepper flakes, or to taste

Since only three ingredients season this colorful spaghetti dish, they should be of the best quality. For the brightest green, chop the parsley at the last moment, and crumble a whole dried chili pepper for bright red. Serve with Grilled Fillet of Bass (page 121).

serves 4

1. Bring a large pot of abundantly salted water to a boil. Add the pasta and cook until al dente; drain.

2. Toss the pasta with the parsley, olive oil, and red pepper. Serve immediately.

linguine with crushed black pepper

½ pound linguine

3 tablespoons unsalted butter, melted

½ cup freshly grated Parmesan, or to taste

1 teaspoon freshly crushed black pepper, or to taste

This is the simplest preparation for pasta there is. The secret is the coarseness of the pepper and the freshness of the Parmesan cheese. Unless you can adjust the grinder on your pepper mill, I recommend crushing the pepper coarsely in a mortar; most pepper mills grind pepper too fine. Grate the cheese at the last moment. This linguine is a perfect balance to heavier main courses such as Veal with Hazelnuts (page 93) or fish dishes such as Parsley-Stuffed Grilled Porgy and Mackerel (page 123).

serves 2

1. Bring a large pot of abundantly salted water to a boil. Add the pasta and cook until al dente; drain.

2. Toss the pasta with the butter, Parmesan, and black pepper. Serve immediately.

spaghetti with red pepper, garlic, anchovies, and parsley

1 pound spaghetti

¼ cup olive oil

6 anchovy fillets, finely chopped

½ cup finely chopped fresh parsley

½ teaspoon red chili pepper flakes

3 garlic cloves, peeled and very finely chopped

This ready-in-minutes dish is excellent with fish. The trinity of garlic, anchovy, and parsley is a classic Italian flavor that I love—and you will too.

serves 4

1. Bring a large pot of abundantly salted water to a boil. Add the spaghetti and cook until al dente; drain.

2. Meanwhile, combine the remaining ingredients in a sauté pan and cook over low heat for 6 to 8 minutes, stirring frequently to keep the garlic from burning.

3. Toss the spaghetti with the sauce. Serve immediately, without cheese. (Cheese is not traditionally served with pastas that include fish.)

fettuccine with anchovy butter

1 pound fettuccine or
   tagliatelle

10 tablespoons unsalted
   butter, softened

12 anchovy fillets

2 teaspoons freshly
   squeezed lemon
   juice

Freshly ground black
   pepper to taste

½ cup finely chopped
   fresh parsley

Butter doesn't figure much in my cooking, but mashed with anchovies over pasta, it's wonderful. Surprisingly, I find that children love this dish. Prepare extra anchovy butter and you can also make Grilled Red Snapper alla Calabrese (page 127), which will then give you a quick but satisfying dinner.

serves 4

1. Bring a large pot of abundantly salted water to a boil. Add the pasta and cook until al dente; drain.

2. Meanwhile, with a fork, mash together the butter, anchovies, lemon juice, pepper, and 6 tablespoons of the parsley.

3. Toss the pasta with the anchovy butter. Serve with a sprinkling of the remaining 2 tablespoons parsley on top.

perciatelli with fried eggs

½ pound perciatelli
(bucatini) or
spaghetti

3 tablespoons unsalted
butter

2 large eggs

¼ cup freshly grated
Parmesan

2 teaspoons freshly
ground black pepper

Finely chopped fresh
parsley (optional)

Perciatelli, also called bucatini, is a thick, hollow spaghetti. Dressed with Parmesan cheese and fresh black pepper and topped with sunny-side-up eggs, this dish makes a nice lunch or late dinner.

serves 2

1. Bring a large pot of abundantly salted water to a boil. Add the pasta and cook until al dente; drain.

2. Meanwhile, a few minutes before the pasta is done, melt the butter in a medium frying pan. When it has stopped bubbling and turns a light brown, crack the eggs into the pan and cook until the whites are set.

3. Toss the pasta with the cheese and pepper. Divide the pasta between two individual bowls and slide an egg on top of each serving. Garnish with chopped parsley if desired.

Note: If you want a greater yield, increase the ingredients proportionally, but serve the pasta on a large platter with the eggs and a sprinkling of parsley on top.

pizzaiola sauce for leftover macaroni

4 to 6 cups cooked
  macaroni

½ pound mozzarella,
  sliced

3 to 4 ripe plum
  tomatoes, chopped

6 imported black olives,
  pitted and chopped

2 anchovy fillets,
  chopped (optional)

2 garlic cloves, peeled
  and finely chopped

1 tablespoon capers

Salt and freshly ground
  black pepper to taste

Olive oil to taste

Dried oregano to taste

A great way to use up leftover cooked macaroni is with pizzaiola, an aromatic sauce of tomatoes, olives, garlic, and oregano.

serves 2 to 3

1. Preheat the broiler. Lightly oil a baking dish.

2. Spread the pasta over the bottom of the baking dish. Layer the cheese on top and sprinkle the remaining ingredients over all. Be generous with the oregano.

3. Broil for 10 minutes, or until the cheese is a light golden brown and the pasta is heated through.

spaghetti with fried zucchini

½ pound spaghetti

Pure olive oil for deep-frying (see Note)

2 medium zucchini, sliced diagonally

2 tablespoons extra virgin olive oil

1 small onion, peeled and finely chopped

1 garlic clove, peeled and finely chopped

Salt and freshly ground black pepper to taste

Handful of fresh oregano leaves, chopped

¼ teaspoon red chili pepper flakes

¼ cup freshly grated Parmesan

Tender zucchini about six inches long are ideal for this preparation. They are sweeter than the large ones, which I find tough and woody. To keep cooking time to a minimum, deep-fry the zucchini while you sauté the onion and garlic.

serves 2

1. Bring a large pot of abundantly salted water to a boil. Add the pasta and cook until al dente; drain.

2. Meanwhile, in a large deep pot or a deep fryer, heat the deep-frying oil to 360°F. Deep-fry the zucchini, in batches if necessary, until lightly browned all over, about 3 minutes. Drain.

3. At the same time, in a large deep skillet, combine the extra virgin olive oil, onion, and garlic and sauté over medium-high heat for 4 to 5 minutes, or until the onion is translucent, stirring frequently. Remove from the heat.

4. Add the zucchini to the skillet with the onion. Add salt and pepper and stir, then stir in the oregano and red pepper flakes. Add the pasta and cheese and toss gently until well mixed. Serve immediately.

Note: If you would rather sauté the zucchini, increase the extra virgin olive oil to ¼ cup. Dice the zucchini instead of slicing it, and sauté along with the onion and garlic.

rigatoni with olives and herbs

1½ cups pitted Sicilian or Greek oil-cured black olives

1 garlic clove, peeled and smashed

½ cup extra virgin olive oil

2 tablespoons chopped fresh oregano

2 tablespoons chopped fresh marjoram

3 tablespoons chopped fresh parsley

½ teaspoon red chili pepper flakes (optional)

1 pound rigatoni

Freshly grated Parmesan (optional)

This is a fast preparation because the sauce is not cooked. The imported black olives cured with oil, salt, and the sun, rather than brine, are a nice contrast in color and taste to the rigatoni.

serves 4

1. In a bowl, combine the olives, garlic, olive oil, herbs, and red pepper flakes, if using. Set aside to marinate.

2. Bring a large pot of abundantly salted water to a boil. Add the rigatoni and cook until al dente; drain. Transfer to a serving bowl and add the black olives with their marinade. Toss gently but thoroughly. Serve immediately, with Parmesan if desired.

Note: You may use any combination of fresh herbs.

penne with tomato, basil, and anchovy

½ pound penne

1 garlic clove, peeled and crushed

¼ cup extra virgin olive oil

1 small onion, finely chopped

4 anchovy fillets

1½ to 2 cups finely chopped ripe tomatoes

4 large fresh basil leaves

Salt and freshly ground black pepper to taste

Pinch of red chili pepper flakes

A glorious dish in summer, when you can pick vine-ripened tomatoes from your garden. Without a garden, or in winter, use imported canned San Marzano plum tomatoes. Remember that the anchovy is used here as a seasoning, to flavor the tomatoes without overpowering them.

serves 2

1. Bring a large pot of abundantly salted water to a boil. Add the pasta and cook until al dente; drain.

2. Meanwhile, in a pan large enough to hold the pasta, sauté the garlic in the olive oil until it just begins to turn light brown. Remove and discard the garlic. Add the onion and sauté over medium heat until golden, about 6 minutes. Stir in the anchovies and cook for 2 minutes, or until they melt. Add the tomatoes and basil, raise the heat to high, and cook for 5 minutes. Add the salt and black and red pepper and cook for 5 minutes.

3. Add the penne to the sauce. Mix well and serve immediately.

penne with yellow pepper, black olives, and tomatoes

1 pound penne or other short tubular macaroni

¼ cup extra virgin olive oil

1 small onion, peeled and finely chopped

1 yellow bell pepper, seeded and finely chopped

1 garlic clove, peeled and finely chopped

4 ripe plum tomatoes, finely chopped

¼ teaspoon red chili pepper flakes

½ teaspoon fennel seed

Salt and freshly ground black pepper to taste

½ cup chopped pitted imported black olives

2 tablespoons finely chopped fresh parsley

Freshly grated Parmesan

A festive dish with colorful flecks of yellow pepper, red tomato, and black olives. Taste your olives for saltiness before you add salt to the sauce. Save time by chopping the onion, yellow pepper, and garlic together.

serves 4 to 6

1. Bring a large pot of abundantly salted water to a boil. Add the pasta and cook until al dente; drain.

2. Meanwhile, in a large frying pan, heat the olive oil over medium-high heat. Add the onion, yellow pepper, and garlic, and sauté for 4 to 5 minutes, stirring often with a wooden spoon so the garlic does not burn. Add the tomatoes, red pepper flakes, and fennel seed and cook for 4 minutes. Season with salt and pepper, and add the black olives and parsley. Cook for another 2 minutes, stirring.

3. Add the pasta to the sauce. Toss well with additional black pepper, and serve with Parmesan.

fettuccine with salsa a crudo

¾ pound fettuccine or
  tagliatelle

2 very ripe large
  tomatoes, seeded
  and finely chopped

½ cup chopped imported
  green olives

2 tablespoons capers,
  chopped

2 teaspoons freshly
  squeezed lemon
  juice

2 garlic cloves, peeled
  and finely chopped

¼ cup finely chopped
  fresh parsley

1 tablespoon finely
  chopped fresh mint

4 anchovy fillets,
  chopped

⅓ cup extra virgin olive
  oil

Freshly ground black
  pepper to taste

A mélange of uncooked ingredients such as olives, capers, and tomatoes, called a salsa a crudo, *is a very quick way to sauce pasta. I suggest serving this dish before or with Grilled Red Snapper alla Calabrese (page 127). If time allows, make the sauce an hour before serving so the flavors can marry.*

serves 2 to 4

1. Bring a large pot of abundantly salted water to a boil. Add the pasta and cook until al dente; drain.

2. Meanwhile, combine all the remaining ingredients.

3. Toss the pasta with the sauce and add additional black pepper, if desired. Serve immediately.

Note: For a more colorful result, if time allows, instead of mixing the sauce at once, add each ingredient one at a time to the pasta and toss. Let sit for 1 hour before serving.

spaghetti with sardines, tomato, and mint

1½ pounds spaghetti

2 garlic cloves, peeled and finely chopped

3 tablespoons finely chopped fresh parsley

¼ cup finely chopped fresh mint

3 cups finely chopped ripe tomatoes

1 4-ounce can sardines packed in water, drained and mashed

1½ tablespoons capers, rinsed and chopped

1 cup extra virgin olive oil

Pinch of salt

Freshly ground black pepper to taste

The salsa a crudo *in this preparation is made from raw vegetables, herbs, and canned sardines. An effortless dish, perfect for a summer's day.*

serves 6

1. Bring a large pot of salted water to a boil. Add the pasta and cook until al dente; drain.

2. Meanwhile, combine the garlic, parsley, and mint. Add the tomatoes, sardines, capers, olive oil, and salt and mix well.

3. Toss the pasta with the sauce, adding abundant black pepper. Serve with crusty bread.

vermicelli with broccoli and sardines

Pinch of saffron

3 tablespoons dry white wine

1 pound vermicelli

2 stalks broccoli, chopped (about 2 cups)

¼ cup olive oil

1 medium onion, peeled and chopped

2 garlic cloves, peeled and chopped

1 4-ounce can sardines packed in water, drained and flaked

2 tablespoons pine nuts

2 tablespoons golden raisins

2 tablespoons water

1 tablespoon tomato paste

Salt and freshly ground black pepper to taste

This is a quick version of a Sicilian favorite. The raisins, saffron, and garlic are the perfect match for broccoli. If this dish is to be a first course, you may want to follow it with Chicken Scallopine with Lobster Sauce (page 108).

serves 4

1. In a small dish, combine the saffron and white wine. Set aside to steep.

2. Bring a large pot of abundantly salted water to a boil. Add the pasta and cook until al dente, adding the broccoli to the water after the pasta has cooked for 5 minutes.

3. Meanwhile, in a frying pan, heat the olive oil over medium-high heat, and sauté the onion and garlic for 5 minutes, stirring so the garlic doesn't burn.

4. Add the sardines, pine nuts, raisins, the saffron with the wine, the water, tomato paste, and salt and pepper; do not stir. Cook until the white wine and water have evaporated, about 4 to 5 minutes, shaking the pan frequently to mingle the flavors. Toss the pasta and broccoli with the sauce, and serve.

spaghetti with chicory and dill

½ pound spaghetti

1 small onion, peeled and chopped

2 garlic cloves, peeled and chopped

3 tablespoons olive oil

1 bunch chicory, washed and chopped

3 sprigs fresh dill, chopped

Salt and freshly ground black pepper to taste

Freshly grated Parmesan

Olive oil for drizzling

Instead of using bitter greens such as arugula, dandelion, broccoli rabe, and chicory exclusively in salads, sauté them with some olive oil and garlic.

serves 2

1. Bring a large pot of abundantly salted water to a boil. Add the spaghetti and cook until al dente; drain.

2. Meanwhile, in a frying pan, sauté the onion and garlic in the olive oil over medium-high heat for 5 minutes, stirring frequently, until the onion is translucent. Add the chicory in handfuls, adding more as it wilts in the pan. Sprinkle on the dill and salt and pepper, and continue cooking for 10 minutes, adding a few tablespoons of water if the pan looks dry.

3. Toss the spaghetti with the sauce and Parmesan. Serve with a drizzle of olive oil.

macaroni con le verdure

1 pound macaroni or ziti

10 ounces spinach, washed, trimmed, and cut into thin strips

2 garlic cloves, peeled and finely chopped

½ cup olive oil

2 yellow bell peppers, cored, seeded, and thinly sliced

1 medium onion, peeled and thinly sliced

Handful of fresh basil leaves, chopped

¼ teaspoon red chili pepper flakes

Freshly ground black pepper to taste

1 cup dry white wine

Extra virgin olive oil for drizzling

Freshly grated Pecorino (optional)

Very fresh vegetables are the key to this dish. If you have any leftover pasta, save it for the frittata on page 142.

serves 4

1. Bring a large pot of abundantly salted water to a boil. Add the pasta and cook until al dente; drain.

2. Meanwhile, in a frying pan, sauté the spinach and garlic in the olive oil over high heat, stirring frequently, for about 3 minutes, until the spinach wilts. Add the yellow peppers, onion, and basil, and cook, stirring, for 5 minutes. Add the red pepper flakes and black pepper, then pour in the white wine and cook until the wine has almost evaporated, about 4 minutes.

3. Toss the pasta with the sauce, mixing well. Drizzle some olive oil over the pasta, and serve with Pecorino, if desired.

macaroni salad with grilled steak and vegetables

½ pound macaroni

¼ pound green beans, cut into ½-inch lengths

½ pound grilled skirt steak or sirloin, thinly sliced

1 small red onion, peeled and chopped

1 red bell pepper, seeded and chopped

1 artichoke heart (fresh or canned), chopped

2 garlic cloves, peeled and finely chopped

3 to 6 tablespoons extra virgin olive oil (to taste)

2 tablespoons finely chopped fresh mint

Salt and freshly ground black pepper to taste

A colorful salad that uses the leftover steak from the weekend cookout. If you have leftover macaroni too, so much the better.

serves 4

1. Bring a large pot of abundantly salted water to a boil. Add the pasta and cook for about 3 minutes, then add the beans and cook for 10 to 12 minutes, until the pasta is al dente and the green beans are still slightly crunchy; drain.

2. In a bowl, mix the steak, red onion, red pepper, artichoke heart, garlic, olive oil, mint, and salt and pepper. Add the pasta and green beans, and toss well. Serve at room temperature.

spaghetti with oregano, bread crumbs, and peas

¾ pound spaghetti

¾ cup fresh or frozen
peas (about ¾
pound fresh peas in
the pod)

¼ cup extra virgin olive
oil

½ cup fresh bread
crumbs

1 tablespoon dried
oregano

Salt and freshly ground
black pepper to taste

*Tossing spaghetti with bread crumbs in-
stead of cheese is a fast and economical
way of seasoning pasta.*

serves 2 to 4

1. Bring a large pot of abundantly salted
water to a boil. Add the pasta and the fresh
peas, if using, and cook until the pasta is al
dente. If using frozen peas, add them about
3 minutes before the pasta is done. Drain.

2. Meanwhile, in a small frying pan, heat
the olive oil. Add the bread crumbs, oregano,
and salt and pepper and sauté for about 4
minutes over medium heat, stirring occasionally. Remove from the heat.

3. Toss the pasta and peas with the bread
crumb mixture, and serve.

tubetti with peas and prosciutto

1 pound tubetti

1 10-ounce package
frozen peas

½ cup extra virgin olive
oil

2 garlic cloves, peeled
and finely chopped

6 tablespoons chopped
fresh parsley

Freshly ground black
pepper to taste

¼ pound prosciutto,
chopped

Tubetti, a small tubular macaroni, works well in this recipe. Keeping the main ingredients similar in size makes it taste better. It's a pretty dish, with green dots of peas and small flecks of crimson prosciutto scattered through the pasta.

serves 4 to 6

1. Bring a large pot of abundantly salted water to a boil. Add the pasta and cook until al dente. About 4 minutes before the pasta is done, add the peas. Drain.

2. Meanwhile, mix the olive oil, garlic, parsley, and black pepper in a large bowl.

3. Toss the pasta and peas with the garlic mixture. Add the prosciutto and toss again. Let sit for 5 minutes before serving.

fusilli with vegetables and herbs

3/4 pound fusilli

6 tablespoons olive oil

1 small red onion, peeled and finely chopped

1 small carrot, peeled and finely chopped

2 scallions, white part with a bit of the green, chopped

1/2 red bell pepper, cored, seeded, and finely chopped

2 garlic cloves, peeled and finely chopped

6 tablespoons finely chopped fresh parsley

6 tablespoons finely chopped fresh mint

2 tablespoons finely chopped fresh dill

1 tablespoon fresh thyme leaves

3 strips cooked bacon, or 2 slices cooked pancetta, chopped

Salt and freshly ground black pepper to taste

Freshly grated Parmesan

This simple dish can also be prepared ahead and served at room temperature. It's a thrifty way to use up all those odds and ends of vegetables in the refrigerator.

serves 2 to 4

1. Bring a large pot of abundantly salted water to a boil. Add the pasta and cook until al dente; drain.

2. Meanwhile, heat the olive oil in a flameproof casserole or frying pan large enough to hold the pasta. Add the red onion, carrot, scallions, bell pepper, and garlic and sauté over medium heat for 8 minutes, stirring occasionally. Add the parsley, mint, dill, thyme, bacon, and salt and pepper and stir to blend. Lower the heat and cook for 4 minutes.

3. Add the pasta to the sauce, and toss well. Serve with abundant Parmesan.

macaroni with beets and mushrooms

¾ pound penne or other short tubular macaroni

Pure olive oil for deep-frying

3 small beets with tops, leaves removed and chopped, beets cut into ¼-inch-thick sticks

½ pound cremini mushrooms, cleaned and sliced

1 garlic clove, peeled and finely chopped

2 anchovy fillets (optional)

3 tablespoons olive oil

Salt and freshly ground black pepper to taste

Freshly grated Parmesan

In this dish of unexpected flavors, beets are fried for a crispy garnish, while the beet leaves are sautéed with mushrooms, garlic, anchovy, and olive oil for an unusual sauce.

serves 2 to 4

1. Bring a large pot of abundantly salted water to a boil. Add the pasta and cook until al dente; drain.

2. Meanwhile, in a large heavy pot or deep fryer, heat the deep-frying oil to 370°F. Deep-fry the beets for 8 to 10 minutes. Drain on paper towels, and sprinkle with salt.

3. While the beets are cooking, in a large frying pan, sauté the mushrooms, garlic, and anchovies, if using, in the olive oil over medium heat for 5 minutes. Add the beet leaves and salt and pepper, mix well, and cook for 3 minutes.

4. Toss the macaroni with the mushrooms and beet leaves. Place the fried beet slices on top and serve with Parmesan.

broken lasagne with portobello mushrooms and pancetta

½ pound lasagne
noodles, broken into
4 pieces each

⅓ cup olive oil

2 ounces pancetta, sliced
into thin strips

1 to 2 garlic cloves,
peeled and finely
chopped

¼ pound portobello or
button mushrooms,
cleaned and sliced

Salt and freshly ground
black pepper to taste

½ cup red wine

12 fresh basil leaves,
finely chopped

Freshly grated Parmesan

Large pieces of broken lasagne noodles make a perfect bed for the rich dark taste of portobello mushrooms. To make the strong flavors even more memorable, add a drizzle of red chili pepper oil (see page 17).

serves 2

1. Bring a large pot of abundantly salted water to a boil. Add the pasta and cook until al dente; drain.

2. Meanwhile, in a frying pan, heat the olive oil. Sauté the pancetta and garlic for 1 minute over high heat. Add the mushrooms and salt and pepper and cook, stirring often, for 6 minutes. Add the red wine and basil and cook for about 4 minutes, or until the wine has evaporated. Keep warm over low heat.

3. Arrange the pasta on a serving platter or on individual plates and cover with the mushrooms. Serve with Parmesan.

spaghetti with broccoli, lemon zest, and almonds

¾ pound spaghetti

1 stalk broccoli, chopped

¼ cup olive oil

Freshly ground black pepper to taste

1 garlic clove, peeled and finely chopped

2 tablespoons finely chopped fresh parsley

Grated zest of 1 lemon

2 tablespoons roasted ground almonds, plus additional for serving (see page 16)

While the broccoli and spaghetti are cooking together, the sauce can be whipped up quickly.

serves 2 to 4

1. Bring a large pot of abundantly salted water to a boil. Add the pasta and cook for 5 minutes. Add the broccoli and cook until the pasta is al dente and the broccoli is tender; drain.

2. Meanwhile, mix the olive oil, pepper, garlic, parsley, and lemon zest together.

3. Pour the sauce over the pasta and toss. Sprinkle the ground almonds over and toss again. Serve immediately, and pass additional roasted ground almonds at the table.

penne with broccoli, fennel, and endive

½ pound penne

1 stalk broccoli, stem sliced, florets separated

¼ cup olive oil

1 small onion, peeled and chopped

½ fennel bulb, trimmed and chopped

2 garlic cloves, peeled and chopped

4 endive leaves, chopped

6 anchovy fillets

Salt (optional)

Freshly ground black pepper to taste

2 tablespoons finely chopped fresh parsley

1 large egg (optional)

½ cup freshly grated Caciocavallo or provolone

A mellow and balanced dish, with the broccoli and fennel, the endive and onion all complementing one another.

serves 2

1. Bring a large pot of abundantly salted water to a boil. Add the pasta and cook for 5 minutes. Add the broccoli and cook until the pasta is al dente and the broccoli is tender; drain.

2. Meanwhile, heat the olive oil in a large skillet that can hold the pasta. Sauté the onion, fennel, garlic, and endive for 5 minutes over high heat, stirring often. Add the anchovies, salt, if desired, and pepper, and cook for 1 minute. Remove from the heat and keep warm.

3. Add the pasta and broccoli to the sauce, along with the parsley, egg, if using, and Caciocavallo. Toss well (if using the egg, toss for about 2 to 3 minutes to cook it), and serve immediately.

farfalle with almonds and artichokes

1¼ pounds farfalle

2 cups chopped roasted red bell peppers (see page 19)

1 cup marinated artichoke hearts, chopped

2 garlic cloves, peeled and chopped

½ cup chopped fresh parsley

Freshly ground black pepper to taste

¼ cup olive oil

½ cup roasted ground almonds (see page 16)

Farfalle is a butterfly-shaped pasta, a shape I particularly like for tossing with chopped vegetables rather than smooth sauces. The roasted ground almonds take the place of cheese in this recipe and make for a crunchy texture.

serves 6

1. Bring a large pot of abundantly salted water to a boil. Add the pasta and cook until al dente; drain

2. Meanwhile, combine all the remaining ingredients except the almonds in a serving bowl.

3. Add the pasta to the bowl and toss well. Add about three fourths of the roasted almonds and toss again. Serve, passing the remaining almonds at the table.

tubetti with ricotta, artichokes, prosciutto, and mint

1 pound tubetti or elbow
macaroni

½ pound ricotta (see
Note)

½ cup olive oil

1 14- to 16-ounce can
artichoke hearts,
drained and chopped

¼ pound prosciutto (in
1 piece), chopped

1 tablespoon finely
chopped fresh mint

2 teaspoons freshly
squeezed lemon
juice

Salt and freshly ground
black pepper to taste

1 small tomato, seeded
and finely chopped

The short tubular pasta called tubetti has the perfect shape to accommodate the chopped prosciutto and artichoke. The dish is flavored with fresh ricotta and mint and garnished with finely chopped tomato.

serves 4 to 6

1. Bring a large pot of abundantly salted water to a boil. Add the pasta and cook until al dente.

2. Meanwhile, mix the remaining ingredients except the tomato in a bowl.

3. Drain the pasta, leaving a little water, and toss with the artichoke mixture. Sprinkle the chopped tomato on top and serve.

Note: Although the commercially produced ricotta available in supermarkets is adequate for this dish, the fresh ricotta made by local cheese makers and sold at Italian markets is far superior.

ziti with lentils, leeks, and almond sauce

½ pound ziti

2 leeks, white part only, washed and finely chopped

1 small white onion, finely chopped

2 garlic cloves, peeled and finely chopped

1 stalk celery, finely chopped

¼ cup plus 1 tablespoon olive oil

1 cup cooked lentils

½ cup dry white wine

Salt and freshly ground black pepper to taste

2 to 3 tablespoons roasted ground almonds (see page 16)

Freshly grated Parmesan (optional)

This preparation begins with a soffritto of leeks, onion, garlic, and celery, a quick way to capture the robust flavors of Italian peasant cooking.

serves 2

1. Bring a large pot of abundantly salted water to a boil. Add the ziti and cook until al dente; drain.

2. Meanwhile, in a large pan, sauté the leeks, onion, garlic, and celery in ¼ cup of the olive oil over medium-high heat for 5 minutes. Combine the lentils with the remaining 1 tablespoon oil and add to the pan, along with the wine and salt and pepper. Cook for 5 minutes longer, and remove from the heat. Add the almonds and mix well.

3. Pour the sauce over the ziti, and serve with Parmesan if desired.

fettuccine with fontina fondue

½ pound fettuccine or
   tagliatelle

2 tablespoons unsalted
   butter

2 tablespoons heavy
   cream

1 garlic clove, peeled and
   crushed

¼ pound Fontina,
   preferably Val
   d'Aosta, diced
   (see Note)

2 large egg yolks

Salt and freshly ground
   black pepper to taste

A rich, creamy, stick-to-your-ribs pasta from the Italian Alps. Serve this with a light red wine or a rosé.

serves 2

1 . Bring a large pot of abundantly salted water to a boil. Add the pasta and cook until al dente; drain.

2 . Meanwhile, pour an inch or so of water into the bottom of a double boiler and bring to a boil over high heat. Put the butter, cream, garlic, and Fontina in the top of the double boiler, reduce the heat to low, and whisk gently until the cheese is melted and smooth. Raise the heat to high and quickly beat in the egg yolks one at a time, beating until the sauce is creamy. Season with salt and pepper.

3 . Pour the sauce over the pasta and toss well. Serve immediately.

Note: If using Fontina Val d'Aosta, include some of the rind of the cheese, which adds a nice texture.

tortelloni with three cheeses

½ pound tortelloni

2 ounces Gorgonzola, crumbled

2 ounces mascarpone

2 ounces Taleggio, diced

Freshly ground black pepper to taste

I use store-bought tortelloni with various fillings in this recipe. Although the three cheeses are delicious, they are quite rich, so serve the pasta with a simple green salad. I like to drink a sparkling white wine with this dish, such as an Asti Spumante.

serves 2

1. Bring a large pot of abundantly salted water to a boil. Add the tortelloni and cook until al dente; drain.

2. Meanwhile, combine the cheeses in a small sauté pan and melt over low heat, mixing gently with a fork or spoon.

3. Toss the tortelloni with the cheeses until well coated. Sprinkle black pepper over the pasta and serve.

perciatelli with three cheeses and two peppers

½ pound perciatelli

½ cup freshly grated Parmesan

3 ounces mascarpone

2 ounces Gorgonzola, crumbled

3 tablespoons finely chopped fresh parsley

Pinch of cayenne pepper

⅛ teaspoon freshly ground black pepper

¼ cup olive oil

This sauce can be prepared in a matter of seconds. The heat of the pasta melts the cheeses just enough to blend the flavors even further. A dusting of cayenne provides a nice bite and a pretty contrast to the creamy colors of the cheeses.

serves 2

1. Bring a large pot of abundantly salted water to a boil. Add the perciatelli and cook until al dente; drain.

2. Meanwhile, mix the remaining ingredients together in a large bowl with a fork or spoon until well blended.

3. Toss the pasta well with the sauce and serve.

spaghetti with parmesan, ricotta, and white wine

¾ pound spaghetti

6 tablespoons ricotta

6 tablespoons freshly
grated Parmesan

¼ cup dry white wine

2 tablespoons olive oil

⅛ teaspoon red chili
pepper flakes

Salt and freshly ground
black pepper to taste

This sauce has a creamy, cheesy texture, thinned slightly with wine. The dish is ideal served with a salad or simple steamed vegetables.

serves 2 to 4

1. Bring a large pot of abundantly salted water to a boil. Add the pasta and cook until al dente; drain.

2. Meanwhile, in a large bowl, mix together the ricotta, Parmesan, white wine, olive oil, red pepper flakes, and salt and pepper.

3. Toss the spaghetti with the sauce, and serve.

perciatelli with ricotta salata and anchovies

½ pound perciatelli

⅓ cup olive oil

1 garlic clove, peeled and
lightly crushed

1 dried red chili pepper

10 anchovy fillets

¼ cup finely chopped
fresh parsley

3 tablespoons freshly
grated or finely
crumbled ricotta
salata, or more to
taste

Freshly ground black
pepper to taste

Ricotta salata is a dry ricotta that is available in two forms, a crumbly one for eating and a hard one for grating. Use whichever is available.

serves 2

1. Bring a large pot of abundantly salted water to a boil. Add the pasta and cook until al dente.

2. Meanwhile, in a small frying pan, heat the olive oil. Sauté the garlic clove and red pepper over medium heat until the garlic just begins to turn light brown. Remove and discard the garlic clove. Reduce the heat to low and add the anchovy fillets. Cook, stirring, until the anchovies have melted. Add the parsley, reserving a little for sprinkling on the pasta, and stir with a fork until well mixed.

3. Drain the pasta, leaving a few tablespoons of water in the pot, and return the pasta to the pot. Sprinkle on the ricotta salata and toss well. Add the anchovy sauce and toss again. Remove the chili pepper, and transfer to a serving bowl. Taste and add more ricotta salata if desired. Sprinkle the top with the reserved parsley and the black pepper.

fettuccine with mint, walnut, and mascarpone pesto

½ pound fettuccine or trenette

1⅓ cups loosely packed fresh mint leaves

⅓ cup walnut halves

2 garlic cloves, peeled

1 tablespoon freshly grated Parmesan

Salt and freshly ground black pepper to taste

⅓ cup olive oil

2 tablespoons mascarpone-Gorgonzola torta or 1 tablespoon each mascarpone and Gorgonzola, mixed together

The famous pesto Genovese is now a familiar dish to many Americans. But a pesto need not always be made of basil, pine nuts, and Parmesan. This mint and walnut combination is a delectable variation of a traditional pesto. The extra richness comes from the creaminess of the mascarpone.

serves 2

1. Bring a large pot of abundantly salted water to a boil. Add the pasta and cook until al dente; drain.

2. Meanwhile, using a mortar and pestle, pound the mint, walnuts, garlic, Parmesan, and salt and pepper to a paste. (You can also use a food processor.) Slowly add the olive oil in a very thin stream as you continue pounding (or with the food processor running). The pesto will take about 8 to 10 minutes, using a pestle, to reach the desired consistency, or much less time with a food processor. If you use a food processor, pulse it in short bursts so that you don't overprocess the pesto.

3. Add the cheese and stir until creamy (do this by hand, not with the processor).

4. Toss the pasta with the pesto and serve immediately.

grilled bluefish, penne, and green bean salad

½ pound macaroni or penne

¼ pound green beans, cut into ½-inch pieces

½ to ¾ pound grilled bluefish (see page 3) or other grilled fish, cut into bite-sized pieces

⅓ cup finely chopped fresh parsley

1 tablespoon extra virgin olive oil

Freshly ground black pepper to taste

The pasta and beans are cooked together in this recipe, saving you time and cleanup. This salad is a great way of using leftover grilled fish. And if you make extra penne and green beans, you can use them to make Macaroni Salad with Grilled Steak and Vegetables (page 39).

serves 2

1. Bring a large pot of abundantly salted water to a boil. Add the pasta and cook for 5 minutes. Add the green beans and cook until the pasta is al dente; drain.

2. Transfer the pasta and beans to a large serving bowl. Add the bluefish, parsley, olive oil, and black pepper. Toss gently. Allow the salad to sit for 15 minutes before serving. Or cover and refrigerate until needed; bring to room temperature before serving.

Note: If you don't happen to have leftover grilled fish on hand, use canned mackerel, sardines, or salmon.

capellini with oysters

½ pound capellini

4 anchovy fillets

⅓ cup olive oil

2 garlic cloves, peeled
    and finely chopped

1 tablespoon capers

¼ teaspoon red chili
    pepper flakes

⅓ cup plus 1 tablespoon
    finely chopped fresh
    parsley

1 pint shucked oysters,
    drained (about 20)

Extra virgin olive oil for
    drizzling

Use already-shucked oysters for speedy preparation. The tart, salty capers and briny oysters swirled together with olive oil, melted anchovies, and garlic work well with angel hair pasta, known as capellini.

serves 2

1. Bring a large pot of abundantly salted water to a boil. Add the capellini and cook until al dente; drain.

2. Meanwhile, combine the anchovies, olive oil, garlic, capers, chili pepper flakes, and ⅓ cup of the parsley in a large sauté pan and cook over medium-low heat for 3 minutes. Turn the heat up to high, add the oysters, and heat for 1 to 2 minutes, just until their edges begin to shrivel.

3. Add the capellini and heat for 1 minute, tossing to mix well. Serve, sprinkled with the remaining 1 tablespoon parsley and drizzled with extra virgin olive oil.

linguine with shrimp, spinach, and lemon

1 cup water

1¼ pounds medium
shrimp (see Note)

6 tablespoons olive oil

2 garlic cloves, peeled
and finely chopped

1 dried red chili pepper,
crumbled

Juice of ½ lemon

1 teaspoon finely grated
lemon peel

1 tablespoon finely
chopped fresh mint

Salt and freshly ground
black pepper to taste

1 ripe tomato, chopped

10 ounces spinach,
washed, trimmed,
and torn into pieces

1 pound linguine

Don't be put off by the number of steps in this recipe: Everything cooks very quickly and the flavorful result is well worth it.

serves 4 to 6

1. Bring a large pot of abundantly salted water to a boil for the pasta.

2. In a small pot, bring the 1 cup water to a simmer. Peel the shrimp, adding the shells to the water, and let simmer for 5 to 10 minutes. Then strain the broth, reserving ½ cup.

3. Place the shrimp in a bowl and add ¼ cup of the olive oil, the garlic, red chili pepper, lemon juice, lemon peel, mint, and salt and pepper. Stir to coat the shrimp.

4. Heat the remaining 2 tablespoons olive oil in a large skillet. Add the tomato and cook over high heat, stirring, for 5 minutes. Add the reserved shrimp broth and cook for another 3 minutes. Add the shrimp mixture and salt to taste. Then add the spinach and cook, stirring often, until the shrimp are cooked through, and the spinach is wilted, about 5 to 7 minutes.

5. Meanwhile, add the pasta to the boiling water and cook until al dente; drain.

6. Place the pasta in a serving bowl and pour the sauce on top. Serve immediately.

Note: If you use peeled cooked shrimp instead of raw shrimp, chop 2 shrimp and combine with ½ cup of boiling water to use in place of the broth. Heat the cooked shrimp for no more than 2 minutes.

linguine with spicy shrimp and peppers

1 pound linguine

½ cup olive oil

1 pound medium shrimp, peeled (see Note)

2 peperoncini, preferably 1 red and 1 green, finely chopped, or ¼ cup each finely chopped red and green bell peppers

4 dried red chili peppers

1 small tomato, finely chopped

2 garlic cloves, peeled and finely chopped

½ cup finely chopped fresh parsley

Salt to taste

1 teaspoon freshly ground black pepper

¼ cup dry white wine

This colorful dish is one of my favorite shellfish and pasta preparations. Chop the peppers, tomato, parsley, and garlic together to save time. The four red chili peppers called for here make for a spicy taste— add even more if your palate can take it.

serves 4 to 6

1. Bring a large pot of abundantly salted water to a boil. Add the pasta and cook until al dente; drain.

2. Meanwhile, heat the olive oil in a large pan over high heat. Add the shrimp, peperoncini, chili peppers, tomato, garlic, parsley, salt, and black pepper. Cook for 3 minutes, stirring so the ingredients cook evenly. Pour in the white wine and cook until it has almost evaporated, about 2 to 3 minutes. Remove the chili peppers and discard.

3. Place the pasta in a serving bowl, and pour the sauce on top. Serve immediately.

Note: If you use peeled cooked shrimp, add them along with the white wine.

spaghetti with herbed garlic and tomato shrimp

1 pound spaghetti

½ cup olive oil

2 to 3 garlic cloves, peeled and chopped

6 tablespoons finely chopped fresh parsley

20 fresh basil leaves, finely chopped

1 tablespoon finely chopped fresh marjoram or oregano

1 tablespoon fresh thyme leaves

1 to 2 dried red chili peppers

⅔ cup dry white wine

1 pound plum tomatoes, peeled, seeded, and chopped

1½ pounds medium shrimp, peeled (see Note)

Salt and freshly ground black pepper to taste

Even though the list of ingredients may look daunting, this is in fact a very quick preparation. Shrimp is ideal with the zesty tomato sauce, abundant with fresh herbs, but a firm-fleshed fish such as swordfish can be substituted. For a hotter taste, add more chili peppers.

serves 4

1. Bring a large pot of abundantly salted water to a boil. Add the pasta and cook until al dente; drain.

2. Meanwhile, in a large frying pan, heat the olive oil. Add the garlic, parsley, basil, marjoram or oregano, thyme, and red chili peppers and cook for 1 minute over high heat. Add the white wine and cook for 3 minutes. Add the tomatoes and continue cooking, stirring occasionally, for 7 minutes. Add the shrimp and salt and pepper. Taste the sauce and adjust the seasoning if necessary. Cook for 3 minutes. Remove and discard the chili peppers.

3. Place the pasta in a serving bowl and pour the sauce over it. Serve immediately.

Note: If you use peeled cooked shrimp, heat for no longer than 1 minute.

Pasta

spaghetti with lobster and hot chili peppers

½ pound spaghetti

3 tablespoons olive oil

5 ounces cooked lobster meat

2 garlic cloves, peeled and finely chopped

¼ teaspoon red chili pepper flakes

10 to 12 large fresh basil leaves, finely chopped

⅓ cup dry white wine

Salt and freshly ground black pepper to taste

Many fishmongers and supermarkets sell cooked lobster meat, making this recipe fast and easy. There is a lot of garlic, red chili pepper, and basil in this dish, but the lobster remains the star.

serves 2

1. Bring a large pot of abundantly salted water to a boil. Add the pasta and cook until al dente; drain

2. Meanwhile, in a small pan, heat the olive oil over high heat for 1 minute. Add the lobster, garlic, red pepper flakes, basil, and half the wine. Sauté over high heat for 1 minute, stirring often. Add salt and pepper, then add the remaining white wine and cook for 1 to 2 minutes.

3. Place the pasta in a serving bowl, and pour the sauce on top. Serve immediately.

Note: If lobster is unavailable, use crabmeat.

do-it-now spaghetti with tuna and capers

¾ pound spaghetti

⅓ cup olive oil

3 garlic cloves, peeled, 1 crushed and 2 finely chopped

1 small onion, peeled and finely chopped

1 6-ounce can tuna packed in water, drained

1 tablespoon capers, chopped

Salt and freshly ground black pepper to taste

¼ cup finely chopped fresh parsley

If ever I was put on the spot, it was when I showed up at my friend Pam's house without the dish I was supposed to have prepared. She had guests, a husband, and two starving kids to feed. There just wasn't enough food and we were going to eat in thirty minutes. I said sheepishly, "Maybe I can whip something up if you have pasta and a can of tuna." She said, in her inimitable way, "Do it now!" So I did.

serves 4

1. Bring a large pot of abundantly salted water to a boil. Add the pasta and cook until al dente; drain.

2. Meanwhile, heat the olive oil with the crushed garlic clove in a large pan over medium-high heat until the garlic just begins to turn light brown, about 1 minute. Remove the garlic and discard. Add the onion and chopped garlic and sauté for 4 to 5 minutes. Add the tuna, along with the capers and salt and pepper. Stir and cook for 1 minute. Remove from the heat and keep warm.

3. Add the pasta to the tuna sauce, along with half the parsley, and toss. Sprinkle the remaining parsley on top and serve.

fettuccine with striped bass and tomato

½ cup olive oil

1 large shallot, peeled and chopped

2 garlic cloves, peeled and finely chopped

3 tablespoons finely chopped fresh parsley

3 tablespoons finely chopped fresh oregano

1 large ripe tomato, finely chopped

Salt and freshly ground black pepper to taste

½ cup dry white wine

1½ pounds striped bass fillets, skinned and sliced into bite-sized pieces

1 pound fettuccine or fettuccelle

Striped bass is a firm-fleshed fish that marries perfectly with this herbed tomato sauce. If I can find it, I like to make the dish with fettucelle, a pasta that is wider than linguine but narrower than fettucini. Catfish, redfish, mahi-mahi, or monkfish can be used in place of the bass. Sweet-and-Sour Celery (page 166) goes well with this dish.

serves 4 to 6

1. In a deep frying pan, heat the olive oil. Sauté the shallot and garlic over medium heat for 3 to 4 minutes, stirring often. Add the parsley and oregano and cook for 2 minutes. Add the tomato and salt and pepper and cook for 3 minutes. Add the wine, raise the heat to high, and cook for 3 minutes. Add the striped bass and cook for 5 to 7 minutes, until the bass is cooked through but still moist. Adjust the salt and pepper if necessary.

2. Meanwhile, bring a large pot of abundantly salted water to a boil. Add the pasta and cook until al dente; drain.

3. Toss the pasta gently but thoroughly with the sauce. Serve immediately, without cheese. (Cheese is not traditionally served with fish pastas.)

spaghetti with swordfish and scallops

½ pound spaghetti

1 small onion, peeled and chopped

2 garlic cloves, peeled and finely chopped

6 tablespoons finely chopped fresh parsley

1 teaspoon fennel seed

3 tablespoons olive oil

½ cup dry white wine

2 tablespoons tomato paste dissolved in 1 cup hot water

1 dried red chili pepper

4 ounces swordfish, cut into scallop-sized pieces (about 1½-inch chunks)

6 ounces large sea scallops

Freshly ground black pepper to taste

Let the seafood mingle with the rich, spicy tomato sauce for a few extra minutes before serving and the dish will be even more flavorful.

serves 2

1. Bring a large pot of abundantly salted water to a boil. Add the spaghetti and cook until al dente; drain.

2. Meanwhile, in a large frying pan, sauté the onion, garlic, parsley, and fennel seed in the olive oil over medium-high heat for about 4 minutes. Add the wine, increase the heat to high, and cook for 3 minutes. Add the tomato paste and water and the red pepper and cook for another 3 minutes. Add the swordfish and scallops and cook, stirring frequently, for 6 to 7 minutes, until cooked through. Remove and discard the chili pepper.

3. Place the spaghetti in a serving platter or bowl and top with the sauce. Add black pepper to taste.

spaghetti with anchovies

1 pound spaghetti

1 cup tomato puree

12 anchovy fillets

½ cup loosely packed
fresh basil leaves

The anchovies in this recipe are used as a condiment, literally disappearing into the tomato sauce. While they are essential, their flavor is balanced by the basil so that they merely season the pasta in a delicate way.

serves 2 to 4

1. Bring a large pot of abundantly salted water to a boil. Add the pasta and cook until al dente; drain.

2. Meanwhile, in a saucepan, heat the tomato puree over medium heat. Stir in the anchovies and basil until the anchovies have melted into the sauce.

3. Transfer the pasta to a serving platter and toss with the sauce. Serve without cheese.

fettuccine with prosciutto and zucchini blossoms

1 pound fettuccine or
tagliatelle

3 tablespoons unsalted
butter

2 tablespoons finely
chopped onion

6 zucchini blossoms,
chopped (see Note)

¼ pound prosciutto,
chopped

1 large egg, beaten
(optional)

½ cup freshly grated
Parmesan

1 tablespoon freshly
ground black pepper

3 tablespoons chopped
fresh parsley

The gorgeous bright yellow blossoms are reason enough to plant zucchini in your garden. The flowers have a delicate, satiny taste and are very pretty tossed with pasta. They can often be found at gourmet green-grocers or farmers' markets. I prefer ta-gliatelle, a pasta wider than fettuccine, when I can find it for this recipe. Serve with Green Beans Wrapped in Prosciutto (page 163) on the side.

serves 4

1. Bring a large pot of abundantly salted water to a boil. Add the pasta and cook until al dente; drain.

2. Meanwhile, in a skillet large enough to hold the pasta, heat the butter. Sauté the onion over medium-high heat for 5 minutes. Add the zucchini blossoms and cook for 1 minute. Remove from the heat and keep warm.

3. Add the pasta to the zucchini blossoms and toss. Immediately add the prosciutto, egg (if using), Parmesan, black pepper, and parsley and toss well. Serve immediately.

Note: If you are unable to obtain zucchini flowers, simply omit them or substitute 1 very small zucchini sliced paper-thin.

fusilli with pork and sweet pepper

1 pound fusilli

⅓ cup freshly grated
Pecorino

¼ teaspoon red chili
pepper flakes

1 large egg (optional)

3 tablespoons olive oil

1 small onion, peeled and
finely chopped

1 garlic clove, peeled and
finely chopped

1 red or green bell
pepper, seeded and
chopped

1 pound pork sirloin or
tenderloin, cut into
small cubes

¼ cup dry white wine

Salt and freshly ground
black pepper to taste

3 tablespoons finely
chopped fresh
parsley

3 tablespoons finely
chopped fresh
marjoram (optional)

This sauce starts with a soffritto of onion, garlic, and sweet pepper, then adds lean pork which is quickly seared. The flavorful result is tossed with fusilli, a corkscrew-shaped pasta.

serves 2 to 4

1. Bring a large pot of abundantly salted water to a boil. Add the pasta and cook until al dente; drain.

2. Meanwhile, in a small bowl, stir together the cheese, red pepper flakes, and egg, if using. Set aside.

3. Heat the olive oil in a large sauté pan and sauté the onion and garlic over medium-high heat for 4 minutes, stirring frequently so the garlic doesn't burn. Add the bell pepper and cook for another 4 minutes. Add the pork and cook, stirring often so the pork browns evenly on all sides, for about 4 minutes. Add the white wine and salt and pepper, and simmer to reduce the wine for 2 minutes. Remove from the heat.

4. Transfer the pasta to a serving bowl. Immediately add the cheese and red pepper mixture and toss well so the pasta is coated. Add the pork and toss again. Sprinkle on the parsley and marjoram, if using, toss again, and serve.

fettuccine with veal marrow and ricotta

½ pound fettuccine

¼ cup veal or beef marrow

1 garlic clove, peeled and finely chopped

¼ cup ricotta, preferably fresh

3 tablespoons freshly grated Parmesan

¼ teaspoon red chili pepper flakes

1 tablespoon finely chopped fresh parsley

Freshly ground black pepper to taste

Marrow is what fills the hollow inside meaty bones. Supermarkets label these bones "soup bones" or "marrow bones." You will be surprised and delighted at the rich, mellow taste. Use a teaspoon or knife to scrape out the marrow, which melts like butter. A small amount goes a long way; what you don't need can be frozen.

serves 2

1. Bring a large pot of abundantly salted water to a boil. Add the pasta and cook until al dente; drain.

2. Meanwhile, combine the marrow and garlic in a small pan and sauté gently over medium heat for 3 minutes.

3. Transfer the pasta to a serving bowl. Add the marrow mixture, ricotta, Parmesan, red chili pepper flakes, parsley, and black pepper. Toss well and serve immediately.

perciatelli with liver, pistachios, and green peppercorns

½ pound perciatelli

3 tablespoons olive oil

2 garlic cloves, peeled, 1 crushed and 1 finely chopped

3 tablespoons finely chopped onion

2 ounces shiitake or cremini mushrooms, cleaned and thinly sliced

10 ounces veal liver, cut into bite-sized pieces

2 tablespoons shelled pistachio nuts

1 tablespoon whole green peppercorns packed in brine

1 sprig fresh rosemary or 1 teaspoon dried

Salt and freshly ground black pepper to taste

5 tablespoons dry white wine

1 roasted red bell pepper (see page 19), chopped

Freshly grated Parmesan

This is a hearty preparation that truly does justice to veal liver. Because liver cooks rapidly, pay close attention to the cooking time—overcooking will make it tough and unappetizingly gray.

serves 2

1. Bring a large pot of abundantly salted water to a boil. Add the pasta and cook until al dente; drain.

2. Meanwhile, heat the olive oil in a sauté pan. Sauté the crushed garlic over high heat until it begins to turn light brown, about 1 minute. Remove the garlic and discard. Add the onion and chopped garlic and sauté for 3 minutes, stirring frequently. Add the mushrooms and cook for 3 minutes, stirring. Stir in the liver, pistachios, peppercorns, rosemary, and salt and pepper. Cook for 1 minute, then add the white wine and cook for 3 minutes. Add the red pepper and cook for 1 more minute.

3. Transfer the pasta to a serving bowl, and ladle the sauce on top. Serve with Parmesan.

penne with kidney and zucchini

½ pound penne or
  macaroni

3 tablespoons olive oil

1 garlic clove, peeled and
  lightly crushed

1 small onion, peeled and
  finely chopped

1 stalk celery, finely
  chopped

2 lamb or veal kidneys,
  chopped

1 zucchini, seeded and
  chopped

1 teaspoon finely
  chopped fresh sage

1 teaspoon finely
  chopped fresh
  rosemary

Salt to taste

¼ cup dry white wine

3 tablespoons grated
  Pecorino Pepato or 3
  tablespoons grated
  Pecorino plus 6
  lightly crushed black
  peppercorns

1 tablespoon finely
  chopped fresh
  parsley

I love veal kidneys and this is a quick way to prepare them. Many people haven't developed a taste for kidneys or even tried them. This is a good introduction for those who are unfamiliar with kidneys. It is important that they be very fresh—if you don't use them the day of purchase, freeze them.

serves 2

1. Bring a large pot of abundantly salted water to a boil. Add the pasta and cook until al dente; drain.

2. Meanwhile, heat the olive oil over medium heat in a skillet large enough to hold the pasta. Add the garlic and cook just until the garlic begins to turn light brown. Remove and discard. Add the onion and celery and sauté about 6 minutes, stirring frequently. Add the kidneys, zucchini, sage, rosemary, and salt, turn the heat up to high, and sauté, stirring frequently, until the kidneys are browned, about 2 to 3 minutes. Add the wine and cook until it has evaporated. Remove from the heat and add the Pecorino Pepato.

3. Add the pasta to the sauce. Toss well and transfer to individual bowls. Sprinkle with the parsley and serve.

spaghetti with tomato, sausage, and rosemary sauce

½ pound spaghetti

⅓ cup chopped onion

1 tablespoon olive oil

6 ounces Italian hot or
  sweet sausages,
  casings removed
  and meat crumbled

⅓ cup dry white wine

2 cups chopped plum
  tomatoes, with their
  juices

2 sprigs fresh rosemary

Freshly grated Parmesan

Thick tomato sauces remind me of my mother's Italian cooking. Bits of Italian sausage and rosemary make this quick version of a traditional sauce flavorful and filling.

serves 2

1. Bring a large pot of abundantly salted water to a boil. Add the pasta and cook until al dente; drain.

2. Meanwhile, in a frying pan, sauté the onion in the olive oil over high heat for 2 minutes. Add the sausage and cook for 2 to 3 minutes. Add the white wine and let it reduce for 1 to 2 minutes. Add the tomatoes and rosemary, partially cover, and cook for 10 minutes, stirring occasionally. Remove and discard the rosemary.

3. Transfer the pasta to a serving bowl, and pour the sauce over it. Serve with Parmesan.

spaghetti with sausage and artichoke mascarpone cream sauce

¾ pound spaghetti

1 tablespoon olive oil

1 tablespoon finely
chopped onion

2 sweet Italian sausages
(about ½ pound),
casings removed
and meat crumbled

2 artichoke hearts (fresh
or canned), chopped

⅓ cup dry white wine

½ cup mascarpone

½ cup heavy cream

6 sprigs fresh marjoram
or parsley and 6
sprigs fresh thyme,
tied together for a
bouquet garni

Freshly ground black
pepper to taste

Freshly grated Pecorino

This substantial recipe is a piatto unico, *an all-in-one dish that's a fast way of getting a warming dinner on the table for a cold winter's night. Serve it with a simple salad, such as Boston Lettuce with Herb Vinaigrette (page 160).*

serves 3 to 4

1. Bring a large pot of abundantly salted water to a boil. Add the pasta and cook until al dente; drain.

2. Meanwhile, in a large deep pan that will hold the spaghetti, heat the olive oil. Sauté the onion over medium-high heat for about 4 minutes. Add the sausage and cook until it loses its pink color, about 4 minutes. Add the artichokes and cook for 1 minute. Stir in the wine and cook for 1 minute, then add the mascarpone, cream, and bouquet garni and stir. Add pepper and simmer for 10 minutes.

3. Add the pasta to the sauce and toss well. Discard the bouquet garni. Serve with Pecorino.

Three

Riso

rice

Rice is particularly popular in northern Italy, where it is often cooked in a flavorful preparation known as a risotto. A risotto begins with a soffritto (see page 19), usually of onions and garlic sautéed in butter. Short-grain rice, such as Arborio or Vialone, is added and coated with the butter. Then a simmering broth is poured in a ladleful at a time while the rice slowly absorbs the liquid and cooks until tender. Parmesan, butter, or other ingredients may then be stirred in, and the final result is a rich and creamy dish.

In southern Italy and Sicily, rice is more often prepared in a style similar to the way Americans cook rice, combining all the ingredients, including the liquid, in a covered pot and simmering, so the grains of rice remain separate.

The first recipe in this chapter is a risotto. The other recipes are for rice that is fluffy with the grains staying separate. Any of the recipes can be completed in about thirty minutes.

rice with parsley and mint

1 cup Arborio rice,
    washed

1½ cups water

1½ tablespoons unsalted
    butter

½ teaspoon salt

¼ cup finely chopped
    fresh parsley

¼ cup finely chopped
    fresh mint

You can chop the herbs as the rice cooks and quickly stir them in at the end. I like to serve this rice, untraditionally, with Steak Pizzaiola (page 91).

serves 2 to 4

1. Put the rice, water, butter, and salt in a heavy 2-quart pot with a tight-fitting lid. Bring the water to a boil. Stir, reduce the heat to low, cover, and cook for 10 minutes. Check the rice: If it is dry and still firm, add ¼ cup boiling water and cook until the rice is tender and the liquid is absorbed.

2. Remove from the heat, and stir in the parsley and mint. Serve.

Note: If you have time, let the rice stand for 10 minutes after you add the herbs to become more flavorful. Lay a paper towel between the pot and lid to absorb the steam instead of letting the condensation drip back into the rice as it stands.

asparagus risotto

1 pound asparagus, trimmed and cut into 1-inch lengths

1 cup chicken broth or 1 chicken bouillon cube

6 tablespoons unsalted butter

1 small onion, peeled and finely chopped

1 cup Arborio rice (do not rinse)

¼ cup dry white wine

Salt and freshly ground black pepper to taste

½ cup freshly grated Parmesan

This creamy risotto is enhanced by home-made chicken broth, but for speed I often use canned chicken broth or a bouillon cube.

serves 4

1. Bring a quart of lightly salted water to a boil. Cook the asparagus for 2 minutes and then drain, saving the cooking water. If using chicken broth, combine it with 1½ cups of the reserved cooking water; if using a bouillon cube, dissolve it in 2½ cups of the asparagus water. Pour the broth mixture into a small pot, and keep it at a gentle simmer over medium-low heat. Discard the remaining asparagus water.

2. In a heavy-bottomed 2-quart pot, melt 4 tablespoons of the butter over high heat. Add the onion and asparagus and sauté for 2 minutes. Add the rice and cook for 1 to 2 minutes, stirring to coat with butter. Pour in the wine and cook until it has evaporated.

3. Reduce the heat to low and pour in a ladleful of the chicken broth mixture. Cook, stirring, until all the liquid has been absorbed. Taste for salt and pepper. Add another ladleful of broth and continue stirring and adding broth until the rice is tender, but still slightly al dente, and creamy. The rice may take anywhere from 15 to 25 minutes depending on the rice you are using.

4. Stir in the remaining 2 tablespoons butter and the Parmesan and serve.

Rice **77**

sage rice with brussels sprouts and sausage

2 tablespoons unsalted
   butter
2 tablespoons finely
   chopped onion
1 to 2 garlic cloves,
   peeled and finely
   chopped
1 cup Arborio rice,
   washed
1½ cups water
½ teaspoon salt
1 teaspoon finely
   chopped fresh sage
¼ pound small Brussels
   sprouts, trimmed
   and chopped
¾ pound sweet Italian
   sausage, casings
   removed and meat
   crumbled
Freshly ground black
   pepper to taste
Freshly grated Parmesan

Many people are not overly fond of Brussels sprouts, but chopping them and cooking them with sage-flavored rice results in an entirely different experience.

serves 2 to 4

1. In a heavy-bottomed 2-quart pot with a tight-fitting lid, melt the butter. Sauté the onion and garlic over high heat for 4 minutes, stirring so the garlic doesn't burn. Add the rice and sauté for 1 minute, stirring to coat the rice with butter. Add the water, salt, and sage and bring to a boil. Reduce the heat to low and cook for 5 minutes. Add the Brussels sprouts and cook until the rice and Brussels sprouts are al dente and all the liquid has been absorbed, 10 to 20 minutes.

2. Meanwhile, in a skillet, sauté the sausage over high heat, stirring with a wooden spoon, for about 10 minutes, or until it loses its pink color. If it starts to stick, add a few tablespoons of water. Using a slotted spoon, transfer to paper towels to drain.

3. Remove the rice from the heat and stir in the sausage and pepper. Lay a paper towel between the pot and the lid and let stand for 5 minutes before serving. Serve with Parmesan.

rice with saffron shrimp

Pinch of saffron

1 cup tepid water

3 tablespoons olive oil

1 small onion, peeled and finely chopped

1 garlic clove, peeled and finely chopped

2 plum tomatoes, finely chopped

3 tablespoons finely chopped fresh parsley

1 cup Arborio rice, washed

¼ pound medium shrimp, shelled and chopped in thirds

Salt and freshly ground black pepper to taste

Rice with saffron is even more delicious when you add shrimp. Don't be tempted to add more garlic here; the amount called for in the recipe is just right. If you like, double the recipe and enjoy the leftovers the next day as a lunch salad.

serves 2 to 4

1. Put the saffron in the tepid water and set aside to steep.

2. Heat the olive oil in a heavy-bottomed 2-quart pot with a tight-fitting lid. Stir in the onion, garlic, tomatoes, and parsley and sauté over high heat for 3 minutes. Add the rice and shrimp and sauté for 1 minute, stirring. Add the saffron with the water and salt and pepper. Bring to a boil, stir, reduce the heat to low, and cook, covered, for 12 to 15 minutes, until the liquid is absorbed and the rice is al dente. Serve.

Note: If you like softer rice, use 1½ cups water and cook until all the liquid is absorbed.

saffron rice alla marinara

Pinch of saffron

1⅓ cups tepid water

2 tablespoons olive oil

2 tablespoons finely
chopped onion

1 garlic clove, peeled and
finely chopped

¼ cup finely chopped
fresh parsley

1⅓ cups Arborio rice,
washed

6 ounces medium
shrimp, shelled

6 ounces sea scallops,
cut in half

2 squid (about ¼ pound),
cleaned and sliced
into rings

1 teaspoon salt

2 dried red chili peppers

Freshly ground black
pepper to taste

This exquisite dish with its colorful specks of saffron and sprinkling of parsley is a treat for the eye as well as the palate. Buy cleaned squid to save time.

serves 2 to 4

1. Place the saffron in the tepid water and set aside to steep.

2. In a heavy-bottomed 2-quart pot with a tight-fitting lid, heat the olive oil and sauté the onion, garlic, and parsley over high heat for 2 minutes. Add the rice and sauté for 1 minute, stirring. Add the shrimp, scallops, squid, and salt and sauté for 1 minute. Add the saffron with the water, red peppers, and black pepper and bring to a boil. Reduce the heat to low, cover, and cook, checking the rice occasionally, until the rice is al dente, 10 to 15 minutes. Serve.

rice with salmon and salmon caviar

2 tablespoons unsalted
butter

1 small onion, peeled and
finely chopped

1 garlic clove, peeled and
finely chopped

3 tablespoons finely
chopped fresh
parsley

1 cup Arborio rice,
washed

1⅓ cups tepid water

1 teaspoon salt

6 ounces salmon fillet,
skinned and cut into
small pieces

3 fresh sage leaves (see
Note)

1 hard-boiled egg, peeled
and very finely
chopped

2 to 4 teaspoons salmon
caviar (optional)

Salmon caviar, while expensive, makes this already luscious dish even more elegant— perfect for a special occasion when you're pressed for time. Salmon caviar can be found in small jars at the supermarket.

serves 2 to 4

1. Melt the butter in a heavy-bottomed 2-quart pot with a tight-fitting lid. Sauté the onion, garlic, and 1 tablespoon of the parsley for 3 minutes, stirring over high heat. Add the rice and sauté for 1 minute. Stir in the water and salt, and then gently stir in the salmon and sage leaves. Bring the water to a boil, then reduce the heat to very low, cover, and cook for 12 to 15 minutes, or until all the water is absorbed and the rice is al dente.

2. Spoon the rice into individual serving bowls and discard the sage leaves. Sprinkle a circle of chopped egg over the center of each serving. Place a dollop of salmon caviar, if using, in the center of the egg. Surround the egg with a circle of parsley. Serve immediately.

Note: If fresh sage is unavailable, omit the sage rather than using dried.

Four

Carne e Pollame

meat and poultry

To make any preparation involving meat, chicken, or duck go faster, ask your butcher to do the cutting and boning work while you do the rest of the shopping. Why waste time trimming off fat, boning chickens, or butterflying steaks when the butcher is willing to do it? Supermarket butcher departments are increasingly aware and responsive to the needs of time-pressed shoppers and offer all kinds of precut and conveniently packaged products.

The meat and poultry recipes in this chapter are for hearty, satisfying dishes. Although many of these dishes go well with pasta, in general I prefer serving red meat with a simple vegetable or side dish and chicken with pasta or rice.

With three kids to feed, I'm a great fan of meatballs. All of the four meatball recipes that follow can be doubled so you can freeze half to have on hand.

meatballs stuffed with almonds, mint, and mozzarella

1 pound ground beef
(ground twice)

2 tablespoons roasted
ground almonds (see
page 16)

3 tablespoons freshly
grated Parmesan

2 large egg yolks

3 tablespoons finely
chopped onion

3 tablespoons finely
chopped fresh mint

Salt and freshly ground
black pepper to taste

2 ounces mozzarella,
preferably fresh,
cubed

Olive or sunflower seed
oil for deep-frying

Flour for dredging

This easy recipe makes meatballs with a nice texture, good served with a trito, *similar to a salsa, of very finely chopped ripe tomato and mint. Serve with pasta or rice. Leftovers are great in sandwiches.*

serves 4

1. In a large bowl, knead together the meat, almonds, Parmesan, egg yolks, onion, mint, and salt and pepper. Take a handful of meat and flatten it into a patty. Place a cube of mozzarella in the middle and enclose it in the meat, forming a ball about 1¾ inches in diameter. Roll it between your palms, and set aside. Repeat with the remaining meat mixture and cheese. Moisten your hands with water to keep the meat from sticking.

2. Meanwhile, in a large heavy pot or a deep fryer, heat the oil to 360°F.

3. Dredge the meatballs in the flour, shaking off the excess. Deep-fry the meatballs in batches for 2 minutes, turning once, until browned on all sides. Drain on paper towels. Serve.

Note: If you prefer, you can sauté the meatballs in a little olive oil instead of deep-frying them. Shake the skillet frequently to avoid sticking.

fried meatballs

1 large slice stale or
lightly toasted Italian
bread or 4 small
slices stale or lightly
toasted French bread

½ cup milk

1½ pounds ground beef
(ground twice)

½ pound ground pork
(ground twice)

2 large egg yolks

½ cup freshly grated
Parmesan

1 small onion, peeled and
finely chopped

½ stalk celery, finely
chopped

¼ cup finely chopped
fresh parsley

Salt and freshly ground
black pepper to taste

Pure olive oil for deep-
frying

Flour for dredging

Chopped fresh parsley
(optional)

The secret to these meatballs is to use good-quality bread and to grind the meat twice. Ask your butcher to grind the meat, or use a food processor and grind the beef and bread together. These go well with Crispy Fried Fennel in Light Tomato Sauce (page 181).

serves 4

1. Dip the bread in the milk, squeeze the milk out, and crumble the bread into a large bowl.

2. Add the beef, pork, egg yolks, Parmesan, onion, celery, parsley, and salt and pepper and knead vigorously. With damp hands, form the mixture into meatballs the size of a small egg.

3. Meanwhile, in a large heavy pot or a deep fryer, heat the oil to 370°F.

4. Dredge the meatballs in the flour and shake off the excess. Deep-fry, turning once, in batches, for 4 minutes, or until cooked through. Drain on paper towels. Serve with a generous sprinkling of parsley if desired.

sage meatballs with marsala sauce

1 pound ground beef

2 tablespoons freshly grated Parmesan

8 tablespoons unsalted butter, at room temperature

1½ tablespoons very finely chopped fresh sage

Salt to taste

Flour for dredging

¼ cup sweet Marsala

These sage meatballs are bathed in a delicious, slightly sweet wine sauce. Serve them on a bed of plain pasta or after Spaghetti with Broccoli, Lemon Zest, and Almonds (page 45).

serves 4

1 . In a large bowl combine the meat, Parmesan, 4 tablespoons of the butter, the sage, and salt and knead until very well blended. With damp hands, form the meat into small meatballs. Roll the meatballs in the flour and set aside.

2. Melt the remaining 4 tablespoons butter in a large skillet. Sauté the meatballs over medium-high heat until they are browned on all sides, about 7 to 8 minutes. Shake the pan often so they don't stick. (If they do stick, loosen them with a few tablespoons of water and a spatula, not a fork.)

3. With a spoon, remove excess fat from the pan and discard. Add the Marsala and cook until it is almost evaporated, about 2 minutes. Serve immediately.

meatloaf stuffed with eggs

1¼ pounds ground beef (ground twice)

1 small onion, peeled and very finely chopped

1 stalk celery, very finely chopped

¼ cup very finely chopped fresh parsley

1 tablespoon very finely chopped fresh marjoram or 1 teaspoon dried

½ cup bread crumbs, preferably fresh

½ cup ricotta

1 tablespoon crushed pistachio nuts

Salt and freshly ground black pepper to taste

3 hard-boiled eggs, shelled

When I have dinner guests during the work week, I like to serve a quickly prepared dish that is pleasing to the palate but also a little more impressive than a "family" dinner. This meatloaf, or polpettone *in Italian ("big meatball"), fits the bill. I blend the ingredients and hard-boil the eggs in the morning, then shape and cook the meatloaf in the evening.*

serves 4

1. Preheat the oven to 400°F.

2. In a large bowl, combine the beef, onion, celery, parsley, marjoram, bread crumbs, ricotta, pistachios, and salt and pepper and knead until very well blended. (The meatloaf mixture can be prepared ahead, covered, and refrigerated for up to 12 hours.)

3. Press the ground meat mixture evenly over the bottom of an 8-inch by 12-inch baking pan. Line up the hard-boiled eggs lengthwise down the center of the meat. Fold and mold the meat over the eggs into a cylinder shape. Pinch the seams securely closed. (The meatloaf can be assembled up to 2 hours in advance, covered, and refrigerated.)

4. Bake for 20 to 30 minutes, until cooked through. Serve hot.

beef tenderloin with cucumbers and mushrooms

2 tablespoons unsalted butter

1 tablespoon olive oil

3 tablespoons finely chopped onion

1 ounce cremini or button mushrooms, cleaned and julienned

½ cup dry white wine

¾ pound beef fillet, from the tail end, cut into small slices

½ cup heavy cream

½ cucumber, peeled, seeded, and julienned

Salt and freshly ground black pepper to taste

Prime beef tenderloin is as soft as butter and can be prepared very quickly, since its flavor is best when cooked rare. This is a rich (and pricy) preparation needing only a simple vegetable or salad. Use a choice cut of tenderloin, sirloin tip, or flank steak if the prime cut is prohibitively expensive or if you prefer your red meat cooked more than medium. Serve with Boston Lettuce with Herb Vinaigrette (page 160).

serves 2

1. In a large pan, melt the butter with the olive oil and sauté the onion for 4 minutes over high heat, stirring constantly. Add the mushrooms and cook for 4 minutes. Pour in the wine and cook until it has almost evaporated. Add the beef and salt and pepper and cook for 3 minutes, stirring.

2. Add the heavy cream and cucumber and stir to mix. Add salt and pepper and cook over high heat for another 5 minutes. Serve immediately.

grilled filet mignon with pancetta and rosemary

4 slices pancetta or 8 slices bacon

1¼ pounds beef tenderloin or sirloin tips, cut into bite-sized pieces

⅓ cup olive oil

½ cup loosely packed fresh rosemary leaves, finely chopped, or 2 tablespoons dried

Salt and freshly ground black pepper to taste

There is little advance preparation with this recipe—just slide everything onto the skewers—but keep your eye on the grill because of possible flare-ups from the pancetta fat. Replace the pancetta with bacon and the beef tenderloin with sirloin tips if you like. Serve with Green Beans Wrapped in Prosciutto (page 163) or Oven-Roasted Tomatoes with Provolone, Pine Nuts, and Oregano (page 172).

serves 4

1. Preheat a gas grill or prepare a charcoal fire.

2. Using 8- to 10-inch bamboo or metal skewers, skewer the pancetta or bacon and beef: Skewer the end of half a strip of unraveled pancetta or the end of a strip of bacon, then skewer a piece of filet mignon, loop the pancetta or bacon around the meat, and skewer the pancetta or bacon again. Continue in this manner until all the meat is used up, using half a slice of pancetta or 1 strip of bacon per skewer.

3. Brush the skewers with the olive oil and roll them in the rosemary. Sprinkle with salt and pepper. Grill for 5 to 6 minutes, then turn and cook for another 5 to 6 minutes. Serve.

spezzatino of veal with peppers and tomatoes

⅓ cup olive oil

2 garlic cloves, peeled and lightly crushed

1 medium onion, peeled and finely chopped

1 cup finely chopped peperoncini (Italian long peppers)

2 ripe plum tomatoes, finely chopped

Pinch of cayenne pepper

Salt and freshly ground black pepper to taste

½ pound boneless veal loin chop, cut into small cubes

1 tablespoon finely chopped fresh sage

½ cup dry white wine

Although this dish is called a stew (spezzatino), it is actually based on a rapid-fire sauté. Here small cubes of veal are seared and then flavored with peppers, onion, tomatoes, herbs, and wine. Serve with pasta, such as lightly buttered farfalle with fresh Parmesan, or rice.

serves 2

1. Heat the olive oil in a frying pan. Sauté the garlic cloves over high heat until they just begin to turn light brown. Remove and discard the garlic.

2. Add the onion and peperoncini and sauté for 4 to 5 minutes, or until the onion is translucent, stirring almost constantly. Add the tomatoes, cayenne pepper, and salt and black pepper and cook for 1 minute. Add the veal and sage and cook until the veal is browned on all sides, about 3 to 4 minutes. Pour in the white wine, lower the heat to medium, and cook, stirring occasionally, for 10 minutes. Check for seasoning and add more salt, black pepper, and/or cayenne pepper if necessary.

steak pizzaiola

½ cup olive oil

2 pounds boneless beef steak, cut into 4 pieces and pounded thin (about ⅛ inch thick)

Salt and freshly ground black pepper to taste

4 garlic cloves, peeled and very thinly sliced

2 pounds ripe but firm tomatoes, peeled and sliced (see Note)

½ cup finely chopped fresh wild oregano or ¼ cup finely chopped fresh oregano mixed with 1 tablespoon dried oregano

½ cup dry white wine

Long ago in Naples, pizzaiola, a pizza-like sauce, was often used to mask the taste of poor-quality beef or horse meat. Now we have good beef readily available, but the sauce is still a delicious complement to the meat. Wild oregano, available in Greek markets, is the secret to this version. If you can't find it, use a combination of fresh and dried ordinary oregano.

serves 4 to 6

1. Preheat the oven to warm (150°F to 200°F).

2. Heat the olive oil in a large cast-iron skillet until it is just beginning to smoke. Add the meat and sear for 1 minute on each side. Transfer the beef to an ovenproof platter and season with salt and pepper. Keep warm in the oven.

3. Add the garlic to the skillet and cook over high heat, stirring constantly, for about 30 seconds; do not allow the garlic to color. Add the tomatoes and sprinkle with salt and pepper and the oregano. Cook for about 8 minutes over high heat, stirring occasionally. Add the wine and cook until it has nearly evaporated. Return the beef slices to the skillet for 1 to 2 minutes. Serve immediately.

Note: You can use canned tomatoes, but the consistency of the sauce will be different.

veal loin with fig, almond, and mint cream sauce

4 tablespoons unsalted
   butter

8 boneless veal loin
   steaks (about 2
   ounces each)

Salt and freshly ground
   black pepper to taste

2 ounces blanched whole
   almonds (about ⅓
   cup)

¾ cup sweet Marsala

¾ cup heavy cream

4 ripe green figs, mashed
   (see Note)

1 teaspoon freshly
   squeezed lemon
   juice

2 sprigs fresh mint,
   leaves removed and
   finely chopped, plus
   2 whole sprigs for
   garnish

You'll be surprised how fast you can prepare this very elegant dish with its almond cream sauce sweetened with figs. Serve with Green Beans with Pine Nuts (page 162) and buttered capellini or boiled potatoes.

serves 4

1. Melt the butter in a large skillet. Sauté the veal over medium heat for 2 minutes per side. Season with salt and pepper, transfer to a plate, and cover to keep warm.

2. Pour off the fat from the pan, leaving just a light film. Add the almonds and Marsala and reduce the Marsala over medium-high heat until most of it has evaporated, about 4 to 5 minutes. Reduce the heat to medium low, add the cream and figs, and cook for 4 minutes, stirring occasionally. Add the lemon juice and salt and pepper to taste and cook for 2 minutes. Add the chopped mint and stir well.

3. Arrange the veal steaks on a hot serving platter. Pour the sauce over them and garnish with the mint sprigs. Serve immediately.

Note: Although fig skins are edible, you may prefer not to use them in the sauce. Scoop the flesh out in that case, and discard the skins.

veal with hazelnuts

6 tablespoons unsalted butter

2 veal rib chops (about 1 pound total)

¾ cup hazelnuts, coarsely ground

Salt and freshly ground black pepper to taste

¾ cup dry white wine

¼ cup Frangelico liqueur

1 tablespoon finely chopped fresh parsley

This rich dish is best prepared with top-quality veal and served with steamed vegetables or a simple pasta such as Linguine with Crushed Black Pepper (page 25).

serves 2

1. Melt 4 tablespoons of the butter in a skillet. Brown the veal for about 2 minutes on each side over high heat. Reduce the heat to medium, add the hazelnuts, and cook, stirring often, for 2 to 3 minutes. Season with salt and pepper and pour in the white wine. Cover and cook from 10 to 15 minutes, depending on the thickness of the veal.

2. Add the remaining 2 tablespoons butter and heat until it melts. Add the Frangelico liqueur and cook for 1 minute. Sprinkle with the parsley and serve.

croquettes of veal with apple, walnuts, and taleggio

1 large egg

1 small McIntosh apple, peeled, cored, and finely chopped

1 pound ground veal

⅓ cup walnuts, lightly crushed

1 ounce Taleggio cheese, finely chopped (or substitute Bel Paese cheese)

2 tablespoons dried bread crumbs

4 fresh sage leaves, chopped

Salt and freshly ground white pepper to taste

2 tablespoons unsalted butter

2 tablespoons olive oil

Flour for dredging

⅓ cup sweet Marsala (optional)

Ground veal (or turkey) is combined with chopped apples, cheese, and walnuts and formed into cylinder-shaped croquettes. Serve with Carrots with Marsala (page 161).

Makes 10 to 12 croquettes

1. Beat the egg in a large bowl. Add the apple, veal, walnuts, Taleggio, bread crumbs, sage, and salt and white pepper, and knead very well. Moisten your hands with cold water so the meat won't stick, and form the veal mixture into croquettes, about 2 inches long and 1 inch thick.

2. Melt the butter with the olive oil in a frying pan over medium heat, and heat until very hot but not smoking. Roll the croquettes in the flour, shake off the excess, and place them in the pan. Cook, rolling the croquettes around in the pan so they don't stick, for about 7 minutes. Add the Marsala, if using, and cook for 3 to 5 minutes, scraping up any browned bits from the bottom of the pan. Serve immediately.

lamb with pancetta, mint, and orange zest

¼ cup olive oil

8 thin slices pancetta, cut into strips

1 medium onion, peeled and cut into strips

1 pound boneless lamb loin, excess fat removed, cut into ½-inch cubes

½ cup dry white wine

Salt and freshly ground black pepper to taste

2 tablespoons finely chopped fresh mint

1 2-inch square piece of orange zest, very thinly julienned

In this preparation, the lamb is seared very quickly and seasoned with fresh mint and orange zest. Serve with Spinach Sautéed in Garlic and Olive Oil (page 164) or Sweet-and-Sour Squash with Mint (page 168).

serves 2

1. Heat the olive oil in a sauté pan. Add the pancetta and onion and sauté over medium-high heat for 3 minutes, stirring constantly. Add the lamb and cook, stirring constantly, until browned on all sides, about 3 minutes.

2. Add the white wine and salt and pepper, increase the heat to high, and cook until most of the liquid has evaporated. Stir in the mint and orange zest and cook for 1 minute, stirring constantly. Serve at once.

gobbets of pork with sweet pepper

3 tablespoons olive oil

1 small onion, peeled and finely chopped

1 garlic clove, peeled and finely chopped

1 red, orange, or yellow bell pepper, cored, seeded, and cut into small bite-sized pieces

1 pound boneless pork loin, cut into small bite-sized pieces

¼ cup dry white wine

Salt and freshly ground black pepper to taste

3 tablespoons finely chopped fresh parsley

3 tablespoons finely chopped fresh marjoram or ½ teaspoon dried (optional)

Gobbet *means "mouthful" or "bite," giving you an idea of the size of the pieces of pork. Serve this dish with spaghetti.*

serves 2

1. Heat the olive oil in a large sauté pan. Sauté the onion and garlic over medium-high heat for 4 minutes, stirring frequently. Add the bell pepper and cook for 4 minutes, stirring.

2. Add the pork and sear until browned on all sides, about 4 minutes. Add the white wine and salt and pepper, and simmer for about 2 minutes. Sprinkle on the parsley and marjoram, if using, stir well, and serve.

butterflied pork tenderloin
with nut sauce

⅓ cup hazelnuts

⅓ cup walnut halves

⅓ cup blanched whole
almonds

4 tablespoons unsalted
butter

1 small onion, peeled and
finely chopped

1 garlic clove, peeled and
finely chopped

1½ pounds pork
tenderloin,
butterflied, pounded
to a ¼-inch
thickness, and cut
into 4 pieces

Salt and freshly ground
black pepper to taste

2 cups dry white wine

1 cup heavy cream

Grated zest of 1 orange

2 tablespoons finely
chopped fresh mint

Ask your butcher to butterfly the pork and pound it thin. This is a rich, rib-sticking dish with a nutty, orange-flavored cream sauce. Serve with plain rice or steamed green beans.

serves 4

1. Grind the nuts fine in a food processor. Set aside.

2. Melt the butter in a large skillet. Sauté the onion and garlic for 4 minutes over medium-high heat, stirring. Turn the heat up to high, add the pork, sprinkle with salt and pepper, and cook for 2 minutes on each side. Pour in the wine and let it simmer for a minute or two. Remove the pork and cover to keep warm.

3. Let the wine reduce for 1 minute, then add the nuts and cook for 1 minute, stirring. Add the cream, orange zest, and mint and cook for 4 minutes. Return the pork to the skillet and heat for 1 minute. Serve immediately.

pork spareribs with artichokes and sweet and hot peppers

2 tablespoons olive oil

1 garlic clove, peeled and crushed

1 small onion, peeled, cut in half, and thinly sliced

1 pound boneless pork spareribs, cut into bite-sized pieces

2 anchovy fillets (optional)

½ cup dry white wine

Sprig of fresh rosemary

Salt and freshly ground black pepper to taste

1 dried red chili pepper, crumbled

1 roasted red bell pepper (see page 19), chopped

2 artichoke hearts (fresh or canned), chopped

Most supermarkets sell boneless spareribs, often calling them country-style ribs. This robust dish has a nice bite from the hot red pepper. Serve over a plate of linguine, passing grated pecorino, or with steamed green beans or broccoli.

serves 2 to 4

1. In a deep enamelled cast-iron casserole or a Dutch oven, heat the olive oil. Sauté the garlic over high heat until it just begins to turn light brown. Remove and discard.

2. Add the onion and sauté for 1 minute. Add the pork and cook, stirring, for 3 to 4 minutes, or until the ribs are browned on all sides. Add the anchovies, if using, and cook, stirring, for about 15 seconds. Pour in the wine and stir and scrape up the browned crust on the bottom of the pan with a wooden spoon until it lifts off. Add the rosemary, salt and pepper, and hot red chili pepper and stir well. Add the bell pepper and artichokes and cook for 5 minutes. Serve hot.

grilled skewers of sausage, orange, and bay leaf

10 bay leaves

½ medium onion, quartered and separated into layers

6 links sweet Italian sausage, each cut into 5 chunks

1 large unpeeled orange, cut into chunks the same size as the sausage

Olive oil for drizzling

Fresh juicy oranges skewered and grilled with sausage are an unusual combination that works. The bay leaves and onion contribute an enticing aroma as you grill. Discard the bay leaves but eat all of the orange, including the peel.

serves 2 to 3

1. Cover the bay leaves with tepid water and set aside to soften.

2. Preheat a gas grill or prepare a charcoal fire.

3. Skewer a piece of onion, a chunk of sausage, a bay leaf, a chunk of sausage, a chunk of orange, a piece of onion, and a chunk of sausage, in that order, onto each of ten 6- to 8-inch bamboo or metal skewers. Drizzle olive oil over the skewers and grill for 20 minutes, turning occasionally. Serve immediately.

sauté of sausage, mushrooms, and artichokes

3 tablespoons olive oil

3 links sweet Italian sausage (with fennel), cut into ½-inch chunks

½ pound shiitake or cremini mushrooms, cleaned, halved if large

Salt and freshly ground black pepper to taste

1 sprig fresh rosemary, leaves removed and chopped, plus 1 whole sprig for garnish

8 marinated artichoke hearts, whole or chopped

2 tablespoons dry white wine

1 tablespoon finely chopped fresh parsley

This fast version of a long-simmering winter stew has strong flavors, for what some people call "comfort" food. I usually make Zucchini with Tomatoes (page 179) as an accompaniment. If it is summertime, you can serve this (and the zucchini) at room temperature, with crusty Italian bread and a chilled white wine.

serves 2

1. Heat the olive oil in a large sauté pan over medium-high heat for 1 minute. Add the sausage and cook, stirring, until browned on all sides, about 4 to 5 minutes. Stir in the mushrooms, salt and pepper, and the chopped rosemary and cook for 10 minutes, stirring occasionally.

2. Add the artichoke hearts and white wine, and cook for 2 minutes. Serve garnished with the sprig of rosemary and the parsley.

quick sausage, pepper, and Chianti stew

¼ cup olive oil

4 garlic cloves, peeled, 1 crushed and 3 chopped

1 large onion, peeled and thinly sliced

1 large red bell pepper, cored, seeded, halved lengthwise, and sliced

1 large green bell pepper, cored, seeded, halved lengthwise, and sliced

2 ounces pancetta, cut into thin strips

1¾ pounds hot or sweet Italian sausage, casings removed and meat crumbled

1 tablespoon dried oregano

1 teaspoon dried savory

Salt and freshly ground black pepper to taste

1¼ cups tomato puree

1 tablespoon tomato paste

1¼ cups Chianti

Don't let the long list of ingredients fool you—it's just a matter of throwing one thing after another into this stew with the rich taste of that classic Italian wine, Chianti. Serve on top of pasta or rice or with a platter of green beans, along with crusty Italian bread.

serves 4

1. In a deep heavy flameproof casserole or a Dutch oven, heat the olive oil with the crushed garlic over high heat just until the garlic begins to color. Remove and discard the garlic. Add the onion, red and green peppers, pancetta, and chopped garlic. Cook for 4 minutes, stirring often. Add the sausage, oregano, savory, and salt and pepper and cook, stirring, for 3 minutes.

2. Add the tomato puree, tomato paste, and Chianti, stir well, and cook for 12 to 14 minutes, stirring frequently. Serve immediately, or let rest, covered, for 20 minutes to blend the flavors before serving.

sausage in sweet-and-sour tomato sauce

1 tablespoon sugar

⅓ cup white wine vinegar

2 tablespoons olive oil

1 garlic clove, peeled, split, and lightly crushed

1 pound sweet Italian sausage, cut into bite-sized pieces

2 cups tomato sauce or puree (see Note)

Salt and freshly ground black pepper to taste

½ cup loosely packed fresh mint leaves, finely chopped

½ cup finely diced Caciocavallo

An easy sausage stew that can be served alone or over spaghetti (in which case it will serve four). Accompany it with Baked Stuffed Zucchini (page 180). Double the recipe if you wish, and save half for the next day's panini.

serves 2

1. Dissolve the sugar in the vinegar.

2. In a large deep flameproof casserole or a Dutch oven, heat the olive oil with the garlic clove over medium-high heat. Sauté the sausage until it is browned on all sides, about 6 minutes. Pour in the vinegar mixture and heat, stirring until it has evaporated, about 3 to 4 minutes. Stir in the tomato sauce and salt and pepper, turn the heat up to high, and cook for 8 to 9 minutes, stirring constantly. (The sauce will sputter quite a bit.) Add the mint and cook, stirring, for 1 minute longer.

3. Remove from the heat, and stir in the Caciocavallo. Transfer to a serving platter or bowl, and let rest for 10 minutes. Remove the garlic, and serve.

Note: If using store-bought tomato sauce, buy plain tomato sauce.

kidneys with fried onions, rosemary, and sage

3 tablespoons olive oil

1 garlic clove, peeled and crushed

1 medium onion, peeled and thinly sliced

1 pound lamb kidneys

Salt and freshly ground black pepper to taste

2 sprigs fresh rosemary, leaves removed and chopped, plus 2 whole sprigs for garnish

10 fresh sage leaves, chopped

1 cup dry white wine

Kidneys are succulent and distinctive-tasting, yet they are not nearly as strong as liver. Make sure they are very fresh and cook them the day you buy them (or freeze them). Supermarkets often sell them by the pair. Cooking them whole keeps them flavorful and juicy. If you have any leftover kidneys, use them in Penne with Kidney and Zucchini (page 71).

serves 2

1. Heat the oil in a frying pan and sauté the garlic until very lightly browned. Remove and discard. Add the onion and sauté over medium-high heat for 3 to 4 minutes or until light golden, stirring frequently. Add the kidneys and salt and pepper and cook for 8 minutes, or until the onion is browned and the kidneys have almost stopped "bleeding"—that is, they have stopped giving up their pink juices.

2. Add the chopped rosemary and sage and cook for 1 minute, stirring well. Pour in the wine and cook until it has nearly evaporated. Serve garnished with the sprigs of rosemary.

furious chicken

1 small onion, peeled and very finely chopped

3 tablespoons tomato paste

3 tablespoons olive oil

1 teaspoon cayenne pepper

Salt and freshly ground black pepper to taste

1½ pounds boneless chicken thighs or breasts

This grilled chicken version of penne all'arrabbiata cooks quickly with thighs and even faster with breasts. Arrabbiata, which means "angry" or "furious," refers to the heat from the hot pepper.

serves 2 to 4

1. Prepare a charcoal fire or preheat a gas grill.

2. Meanwhile, stir together the onion, tomato paste, olive oil, cayenne, and salt and pepper until well blended.

3. Flatten the chicken thighs or breasts by pounding gently with the side of a mallet. Coat the chicken with the tomato paste mixture. Grill, turning once, for about 20 to 23 minutes for thighs, about 15 minutes for breasts, basting occasionally with any remaining sauce. Serve.

rosemary chicken with sausage

1/4 cup olive oil

2 garlic cloves, peeled and lightly crushed

1 medium onion, peeled, quartered, and separated into layers

1/2 pound pork rind, cut into thin strips (see Note)

2 ounces prosciutto, cut into thin strips

1 pound sweet Italian sausage, cut into bite-sized pieces

1 1/2 pounds boneless skinless chicken breasts, cut into bite-sized pieces

4 peperoncini (Italian long peppers), cored, seeded, and sliced lengthwise into strips

Salt and freshly ground black pepper to taste

3/4 cup tomato puree

3/4 cup red wine

8 sprigs fresh rosemary, tied into a bouquet

Combining chicken and sausage is typical of home cooking in southern Italy. Every household has a different recipe for this dish. I like to serve it with spaghetti or Sautéed Red Swiss Chard (page 165).

serves 4 to 6

1. In a deep skillet, heat the olive oil. Sauté the garlic cloves over medium-high heat until they just begin to turn brown. Remove and discard. Add the onion, pork rind, prosciutto, and sausage and sauté for 10 minutes, stirring occasionally. With a large spoon, remove any excess fat from the skillet.

2. Turn the heat up to high and add the chicken, peppers, and salt and pepper. Sauté for 3 minutes, turning the chicken often. Pour in the tomato puree, wine, and rosemary and continue cooking until the sauce is as thick as you like it, from 10 to 17 minutes. Remove and discard the rosemary, and serve immediately.

Note: Ask the supermarket butcher for pork rind if it is not in the display case, or buy a chunk of salt pork or pork fatback and cut it off yourself.

spezzatino of chicken with peppers, rosemary, and wine

½ cup olive oil

1 small onion, peeled and chopped

2 garlic cloves, peeled and chopped

5 green bell peppers, cored, seeded, and sliced

1 red bell pepper, cored, seeded, and sliced

5 peperoncini (Italian long peppers), cored, seeded, and sliced

3 tablespoons chopped fresh parsley

1 tablespoon fresh rosemary leaves

Salt and freshly ground black pepper to taste

1½ pounds boneless skinless chicken breasts, cut into 1-inch chunks

½ cup dry white wine

This rustic stew can be an all-in-one meal, a piatto unico, *when served with pasta.*

serves 4

1. Heat the olive oil in a large deep skillet. Stir in the onion, garlic, bell peppers, peperoncini, parsley, rosemary, and salt and pepper and cook over high heat for about 6 to 7 minutes, stirring frequently.

2. Add the chicken and sauté for 3 to 4 minutes. Pour in the white wine and cook until the wine has evaporated, about 10 minutes. If, after 10 minutes, there is still a good amount of liquid left, remove the chicken and peppers with a slotted spoon and reduce the broth over high heat. Return the chicken and peppers and heat for 1 minute. Remove and serve.

spezzatino of chicken and squid

¼ cup olive oil

1 small onion, peeled and chopped

2 garlic cloves, peeled and chopped

2 ounces pancetta, cut into strips

1 pound boneless skinless chicken breasts, cut into strips or bite-sized pieces

1 pound squid, cleaned and cut into strips or rings

Salt and freshly ground black pepper to taste

½ cup dry white wine

1 cup chopped ripe plum tomatoes

1½ tablespoons golden raisins

1½ tablespoons pine nuts

1½ tablespoons dried oregano

1 cup frozen peas

An unusual stew can be quickly prepared by using boneless chicken breasts and already cleaned squid.

serves 4 to 6

1. In an enameled cast-iron casserole, heat the olive oil over medium-high heat. Sauté the onion, garlic, and pancetta until the onion is translucent, about 5 minutes. Add the chicken, squid, and salt and pepper and cook for 2 minutes. Pour in the wine and cook for another 2 minutes.

2. Add the tomatoes, raisins, pine nuts, oregano, and peas, lower the heat to a simmer, and cook for 10 to 12 minutes, uncovered, stirring occasionally. Serve immediately.

chicken scallopine with lobster sauce

4 boneless skinless
chicken breast
halves (8 ounces
each), pounded to a
¼-inch thickness

Salt and freshly ground
black pepper to taste

Flour for dredging

6 ounces cooked lobster
meat, very finely
chopped

¼ cup red wine vinegar

½ cup finely chopped
fresh parsley

1 cup olive oil

6 garlic cloves, peeled, 4
finely chopped and 2
crushed

Ask the butcher to pound the chicken as thin as veal scallopine. The chicken is seared quickly to a golden brown and the lobster sauce is prepared separately. A simple steamed vegetable is the perfect accompaniment.

serves 4 to 6

1. Season the chicken breasts with salt and pepper. Dredge in flour, shaking off the excess, and set aside.

2. In a small bowl, mix together the lobster, vinegar, and parsley. Set aside.

3. In a small sauté pan, heat ½ cup of the olive oil and sauté the chopped garlic over medium-high heat for 1 minute. Add the lobster mixture and cook, stirring frequently, for 4 minutes. Season with more salt and pepper if you like. Set aside, covering to keep warm.

4. Heat the remaining ½ cup olive oil in a large frying pan. Sauté the crushed garlic cloves over medium-high heat until they just begin to turn light brown. Discard the garlic. Sauté the chicken breasts until they are golden on the bottom, about 3 minutes, then flip and sauté for 3 minutes longer. Remove the breasts to a platter and spoon the lobster sauce over them. Serve immediately.

braciola of chicken
with mozzarella and herbs

1 small garlic clove, peeled

1 teaspoon fresh thyme

¼ cup loosely packed fresh oregano leaves

4 ounces mozzarella, finely chopped

4 boneless skinless chicken breast halves (about 1½ pounds)

Salt and freshly ground black pepper to taste

Pure olive oil for deep-frying

Flour for dredging

2 large eggs, beaten

Bread crumbs for dredging.

4 anchovy fillets (optional)

Chopped fresh parsley

Crunchy on the outside, succulent on the inside, this is similar to chicken Kiev. For ease of preparation, ask the butcher to flatten the chicken breasts. Serve with Red Peppers with Capers, Anchovies, and Marjoram (page 171).

serves 4

1. Chop the garlic, thyme, and oregano together. Add the cheese and mix well.

2. Using a mallet, pound the chicken breasts between sheets of wax paper to a thickness of ⅛ inch. Season with salt and pepper.

3. Place a quarter of the cheese mixture on one end of each breast. Roll the chicken up tightly, squeezing gently between your palms.

4. Meanwhile, in a large heavy pot or a deep fryer, heat the oil to 360°F.

(continued)

5. Dredge the chicken breasts in the flour, coating on all sides, and pat off any excess flour. Dip into the beaten eggs, and dredge in the bread crumbs. Then dip in the eggs again and roll once again in the bread crumbs.

6. Place the chicken breasts in the hot oil, adding them one at a time. Deep-fry, turning the breasts carefully with tongs, for 12 to 15 minutes, or until a deep golden brown. The inside of the chicken should be thoroughly cooked. To test, check one breast after 12 minutes by making a small incision with a sharp knife; if it is still pink inside, patch the hole with some bread crumbs and cook for several more minutes. Remove the breasts in the order you put them into the oil, and drain on paper towels. Serve topped with the anchovies, if desired, and a sprinkling of parsley.

turkey scallopine with sage, olives, tomato, and fontina

8 turkey breast fillets, flattened (1¼ to 1½ pounds)

Salt and freshly ground black pepper to taste

¼ cup fresh ricotta

½ cup chopped green olives

16 fresh sage leaves, finely chopped

1 large ripe tomato, cut into 8 slices

¼ lemon

Olive oil for drizzling

½ pound Fontina, sliced

Arrange the turkey scallopine in a baking pan, layer the remaining ingredients on top, and broil for 12 minutes—that's it!

serves 4

1. Preheat the broiler. Lightly oil the bottom of a broiling tray or pan.

2. Arrange the turkey scallopine on the broiling tray. Season with salt and pepper. Spread the ricotta evenly over the turkey. Sprinkle the olives on, then the sage. Put a slice of tomato on top. Give each scallopine a little squeeze of lemon and a sprinkle of olive oil. Lay the Fontina on top.

3. Broil for about 12 minutes, or until the Fontina begins to be speckled with brown. Serve immediately.

turkey breast fritters

Pure olive oil for deep-frying

2 large eggs, beaten

Salt and freshly ground black pepper to taste

1 teaspoon very finely chopped fresh sage (optional)

1¾ pounds boneless skinless turkey breasts, cut into bite-sized pieces

Flour for dredging

Bread crumbs for dredging

Lemon wedges

Chopped fresh parsley (optional)

These crunchy nuggets are a favorite with my kids. You can also make them with chicken. Serve with a wedge of lemon and a sprinkling of parsley, with red pepper oil (see page 17), or with a simple dipping sauce of olive oil, lemon juice, and oregano.

serves 4

1. In a large deep pot or a deep fryer, heat the oil to 370°F.

2. Meanwhile, in a shallow dish, combine the eggs, salt and pepper, and sage, if using. Roll the turkey pieces in the flour, shaking off the excess. Dip in the eggs, then roll in the bread crumbs until well coated.

3. Deep-fry the turkey for 2 minutes, or until golden brown. Drain on paper towels. Serve immediately, with lemon wedges and a sprinkle of parsley if desired.

duck with tangerine sauce

4 tablespoons unsalted
butter

Zest of 1 tangerine, very
thinly julienned

1 5- to 6-pound duck,
meat cut off the
bones, fat and skin
removed, and cut
into slices (see Note)

Salt and freshly ground
black pepper to taste

Juice of 1 tangerine
(about ¼ cup)

½ cup sweet Marsala

1 tablespoon finely
chopped fresh mint

Duck is inexpensive but, unfortunately, often sold frozen—not very convenient for cucina rapida. Occasionally, however, my supermarket will have a defrosted one and then I ask the butcher to bone it and cut it up so I can make this luscious dish.

Many people shy away from duck because of the fat, but it is easy to take care of. Ask the butcher to remove it or do it yourself: Just pull, cut, and scrape the fat out before you cook the duck; if there is any remaining after you cook it, discard it.

This dish also can be made with boneless chicken or turkey thighs. It is excellent with Carrots with Marsala (page 161).

serves 2

1. Melt 1 tablespoon of the butter in a small sauté pan. Sauté the tangerine zest over medium-high heat for 1 to 2 minutes. Remove and set aside.

2. Melt 2 tablespoons of the butter in a medium frying pan. Sauté the duck leg and thigh meat for 4 minutes over medium-high heat, turning often. Add the breast meat and

(continued)

Meat and poultry

salt and pepper and sauté, turning often, for 4 minutes. Pour in the tangerine juice and Marsala and cook for 1 minute. Add the remaining 1 tablespoon butter and cook until the sauce has reduced to the consistency of a thin gravy, about 2 minutes.

3. Stir in the tangerine zest and mint and cook for 2 to 3 minutes. Serve immediately.

Note: If you must bone the duck yourself, and you are not adept at boning fowl, this dish will probably take longer than thirty minutes. But rest assured, you will not be disappointed for your work. Save the bones, wings, and gizzard for making stock or soup.

Five

Pesce e Frutti di Mare

fish and shellfish

Fish is often my first choice for a *cucina rapida* meal. Fish is light, healthful, and cooks very quickly whether you grill, broil, fry, or steam it. Very fresh fish hardly needs a sauce or other accompaniment. The key is freshness.

In these recipes, I call for several different kinds of fish that you may or may not be able to get fresh. Feel free to substitute any similar fresh fish. Experiment with different species: You will be surprised at how good and inexpensive many underutilized fish are.

swordfish croquettes in tomato sauce

14 ounces swordfish steaks, skin removed

2 to 3 tablespoons bread crumbs

1 large egg, beaten

1 tablespoon freshly grated Pecorino

1 teaspoon golden raisins

1 teaspoon pine nuts

Salt and freshly ground black pepper to taste

Flour for dredging

1 cup olive oil

1 garlic clove, peeled and crushed

1 cup tomato puree

Chopped fresh parsley

This recipe is one time when using a food processor is definitely much faster and easier than preparing it by hand. The pureed swordfish is formed into sausage shapes and simmered in tomato sauce. Served over pasta, this makes a complete meal.

serves 2 to 4

1. In a food processor puree the swordfish to a coarse paste. Transfer to a bowl. Or mash the swordfish in a bowl, using the back of a wooden spoon or a pestle.

2. Add 2 tablespoons of the bread crumbs, the egg, Pecorino, raisins, and pine nuts, and mix thoroughly. The mixture should have a doughy, pasty consistency; add another tablespoon of bread crumbs if necessary. Lightly season with salt and pepper.

3. Form the fish mixture into 8 to 10 small sausage-shaped croquettes. (You can prepare the croquettes to this point and freeze for later use.) Dredge the croquettes in the flour.

4. In a 10-inch frying pan, heat the olive oil over medium heat. Fry the croquettes for 3 minutes per side, or until golden brown. Remove with a slotted spoon to paper towels.

5. Drain off half the cooking oil. In the oil remaining in the pan, sauté the garlic clove over medium heat until almost golden. Remove and discard the garlic. Carefully pour the tomato puree into the oil. (It will spurt and splatter.) Stir, and season with salt and pepper. Add the croquettes and cook for about 6 minutes, moving them around in the pan so they do not stick. Serve hot, with parsley as a garnish.

grilled swordfish with orange and thyme

¼ cup olive oil

Juice of 2 oranges

1 bay leaf, crumbled

1 garlic clove, peeled and finely chopped

10 ounces swordfish steaks, about ¾ inch thick

3 tablespoons fresh thyme leaves or 1 tablespoon dried

Salt and freshly ground black pepper to taste

The firm flesh of swordfish is perfect for grilling. While this recipe calls for marinating the fish, it's really more like "flavor-imbuing."

For a grilled dessert, keep the fire going and try Grilled Bananas with Peach Schnapps (page 186).

serves 2

1. Prepare a charcoal fire or preheat a gas grill.

2. Meanwhile in a ceramic or glass baking pan, combine the olive oil, orange juice, bay leaf, and garlic and swish it around. Place the swordfish steaks in this marinade and sprinkle both sides with the thyme and salt and pepper. Let marinate for 20 minutes.

3. Grill the swordfish for 5 minutes on each side, basting with the marinade. Serve.

Note: If you have time, let the swordfish marinate for up to 2 hours.

grilled swordfish
with sammurigghiu sauce

½ cup olive oil

Juice of 1 lemon

2 tablespoons hot water

Salt and freshly ground
  black pepper to taste

2 tablespoons very finely
  chopped fresh
  oregano or 1
  teaspoon dried

6 tablespoons very finely
  chopped fresh
  parsley

2 garlic cloves, peeled
  and very finely
  chopped

1½ pounds swordfish
  steaks, about ¾ inch
  thick

Sammurigghiu *is a Sicilian word that lit-erally means "brine," but here indi-cates a delicious warm sauce made by whipping together olive oil, lemon juice, garlic, and herbs.*

serves 4 to 6

1. Prepare a charcoal fire or preheat a gas grill.

2. Pour an inch or so of water into the bottom of a double boiler and bring to a boil. Pour the olive oil into the top of the double boiler and slowly whisk in the lemon juice and hot water. Season with salt and pepper and then whisk in the oregano, parsley, and garlic. Cook for 5 minutes, whisking con-stantly. Remove from the heat and keep warm.

3. Salt and pepper the fish and grill for about 5 minutes per side. If you like, you can baste the swordfish with some of the *sammurigghiu* sauce, using a brush made of fresh oregano sprigs. Serve the fish, pass-ing the sauce on the side.

swordfish pizzaiola

1¾ pounds swordfish
  steaks

½ pound mozzarella, cut
  into small pieces

½ cup chopped pitted
  imported black olives

2 ounces capers

2 garlic cloves, peeled
  and chopped

¾ pound ripe plum
  tomatoes, sliced

Olive oil for drizzling

Dried oregano

Salt and freshly ground
  black pepper to taste

This is another quick and easy preparation where all the ingredients are layered in a pan and then baked for just fifteen minutes. This swordfish goes well with Tubetti with Peas and Prosciutto (page 41).

serves 4 to 6

1. Preheat the oven to 425°F.

2. Slice the swordfish into finger-sized pieces. Arrange the fish in an oiled baking pan. Sprinkle the mozzarella, olives, capers, and garlic over the fish. Place the tomatoes on top. Drizzle with olive oil, and sprinkle with abundant oregano. Season lightly with salt and pepper. Bake for 15 minutes. Serve hot.

grilled fillet of bass

2 garlic cloves, peeled

¼ cup olive oil

5 sprigs fresh sage, tied
together for a
basting brush

1 pound firm-fleshed
white fish fillets,
about 1 inch thick

Salt and freshly ground
black pepper to taste

The secret to this simple recipe is incredibly fresh fish. The bass can be replaced with any firm white-fleshed fish such as swordfish, monkfish, or catfish. Serve with Spaghetti with Olive Oil, Parsley, and Red Chili Pepper (page 24).

serves 2 to 4

1. Prepare a charcoal fire or preheat a gas grill.

2. Using a mortar and pestle, or the back of a wooden spoon, mash the garlic into a paste. Stir in the olive oil.

3. Using the sage brush, brush both sides of the fish fillets with the garlic and oil mixture. Season with salt and pepper. Place skin side down on the grill and grill for 10 minutes, basting constantly with the garlic oil until just cooked through. Serve immediately.

salmon with tomato, mint, and garlic

6 ripe plum tomatoes, seeded and drained

½ cup loosely packed fresh mint leaves

2 garlic cloves, peeled

¼ cup extra virgin olive oil

Salt and freshly ground black pepper to taste

Olive oil for grilling

1½ pounds salmon fillet, cut into 4 pieces

The salsa a crudo *of tomato, garlic, and mint is best made in a food processor, which whips it into a froth very quickly.*

serves 4

1. Preheat a gas grill or prepare a charcoal fire.

2. Place the tomatoes, mint leaves, garlic, and extra virgin olive oil in the food processor and process until frothy, about 30 to 45 seconds. Add salt and pepper and pulse to blend.

3. Oil the salmon on both sides and season with salt and pepper. Place skin side down on the grill and grill for 4 to 5 minutes. Flip with a spatula and grill for 3 to 5 minutes longer, depending on the thickness of the fish. Serve immediately, with the *salsa a crudo* on the side.

parsley-stuffed grilled porgy and mackerel

12 sprigs fresh parsley

2 1-pound mackerel, cleaned and gutted, tails and fins removed, heads left on

2 1-pound porgies (scup), cleaned and gutted, tails and fins removed, heads left on

¼ cup olive oil

Juice of ½ lemon

Salt and freshly ground black pepper to taste

2 tablespoons finely chopped fresh mint

These two small fish are ideal for a fast grill. I like the contrast between the mild-tasting white flesh of the porgy, also called scup, and the darker, denser meat of the mackerel. Since half the weight of a whole fish is lost in the trimming, these four pounds of fish will yield two pounds or less of fillets.

serves 4

1. Preheat a gas grill or prepare a charcoal fire.

2. Stuff 3 parsley sprigs into the cavity of each fish. Rub with the oil and lemon juice. Sprinkle with salt and pepper.

3. Grill for about 8 minutes per side, until just cooked through. Serve sprinkled with the mint.

Note: You may find it easier to use a fish grill to grill these small fish.

grilled bluefish with oregano, red pepper, and olive oil

½ cup olive oil

3 garlic cloves, peeled and mashed

¼ cup finely chopped fresh oregano or 1 tablespoon dried

1 dried red chili pepper, crumbled

Salt and freshly ground black pepper to taste

1½ pounds bluefish fillets, about ¾ inch thick

Bluefish is a strong dark-fleshed fish that is excellent grilled. When "the blues are running," they're great with a plate of linguine. Save any leftover grilled fish to make Grilled Bluefish, Penne, and Green Bean Salad (page 56).

serves 4

1. Preheat a gas grill or prepare a charcoal fire. Lightly brush the grill with some of the olive oil.

2. Stir together the remaining olive oil, the garlic, oregano, red chili pepper, and salt and pepper. Coat the bluefish generously with this mixture. Lay the fish skin side down on the grill and grill for 5 to 6 minutes, basting occasionally with the remaining oregano and oil mixture. With a spatula, carefully flip the fish over and grill for 5 to 6 minutes longer, basting occasionally. Remove to a platter and serve.

Note: If you serve the bluefish on top of plain linguine, pour any remaining marinade on top.

bluefish braised in wine and fresh oregano

1½ pounds bluefish fillets

Flour for dredging

¾ cup plus 2 tablespoons olive oil

2 garlic cloves, peeled and lightly crushed

2 cups loosely packed fresh oregano leaves, finely chopped

¼ cup dry white wine

¼ cup water

Salt and freshly ground black pepper to taste

Quickly frying the bluefish seals in all its flavor, then braising it in wine, oregano, and water allows the different tastes to mingle. It's delicious and goes well with rice.

serves 4

1. Slice the bluefish fillets into 2-inch by 2-inch chunks. Pat the fish dry with paper towels and then dredge the fillets in the flour, shaking off the excess.

2. Heat the ¾ cup olive oil in a large frying pan over high heat until very hot but not smoking. Sauté 1 of the crushed garlic cloves until it just begins to turn light brown. Remove and discard.

3. Carefully place the bluefish pieces in the pan and fry for 2 minutes, or until golden on the bottom. Flip with tongs and cook for another 2 minutes. Drain on paper towels.

4. Heat the remaining 2 tablespoons olive oil in a sauté pan over medium heat. Add the remaining garlic clove and cook just until it begins to turn light brown. Remove and discard. Place the bluefish in the pan, and add the oregano, white wine, water, and salt and pepper. Cover and cook for about 5 minutes over medium-low heat. Serve with the sauce ladled over.

baked red snapper
with pantelleria sauce

1 pound red snapper
  fillets

Salt and freshly ground
  black pepper to taste

1 medium onion, peeled
  and finely chopped

1 celery heart or 2 large
  stalks, finely
  chopped

1 peperoncino (Italian
  long pepper), cored,
  seeded, and finely
  chopped

3 tablespoons olive oil

6 ripe plum tomatoes,
  peeled and finely
  chopped

1 tablespoon capers

1 tablespoon golden
  raisins

1 tablespoon pine nuts

The aromatic sauce of celery, capers, golden raisins, onion, and tomatoes can be prepared while the fish bakes. This sauce is typical of Pantelleria, an island off Sicily famous for its capers. Serve with Spaghetti with Red Pepper, Garlic, Anchovies, and Parsley (page 26).

serves 2 to 4

1. Preheat the oven to 400°F.

2. Place the snapper in a lightly oiled baking pan. Season with salt and pepper. Bake for 15 to 20 minutes, or just until the fish flakes easily.

3. While the fish is baking, sauté the onion, celery, and green pepper in the olive oil over medium heat for 6 minutes. Add the tomatoes, capers, raisins, pine nuts, and salt and pepper and cook, stirring, for 7 to 8 minutes.

4. With a spatula, transfer the fish to a platter. Cover with the sauce, and serve.

grilled red snapper alla calabrese

2 1½-pound red snapper, cleaned and gutted, heads and tails left on

Olive oil for grilling

Freshly ground black pepper to taste

16 anchovy fillets (about 2 ounces)

4 tablespoons unsalted butter, softened

¼ cup chopped fresh parsley

1¼ teaspoons freshly squeezed lemon juice

Simply grilled and then coated with anchovy butter, these fish can be served with Fettuccine with Anchovy Butter (page 27) for a fast dinner. Mackerel can also be used in this recipe.

serves 2 to 4

1. Preheat a gas grill or prepare a charcoal fire.

2. Rub the fish with olive oil and season with pepper. (It's not necessary to salt the fish, because the anchovy butter is salty.) Grill the fish for 8 to 9 minutes, then turn the fish, using a spatula, and grill about 8 to 10 minutes longer. (The rule of thumb is to grill fish 10 minutes per inch of thickness, measured at its thickest part. A 1½-pound red snapper will take about 17 to 18 minutes.)

3. Meanwhile, mash the anchovies, butter, 3 tablespoons of the parsley, and the lemon juice together in a small bowl.

4. Place half the anchovy butter on top of each fish, spreading the butter so it coats the fish. Sprinkle with the remaining 1 tablespoon parsley and serve.

Note: You may find it easier to use a fish grill for grilling these small whole fish.

redfish with capers and anchovies in white wine

1 small onion, peeled and finely chopped

1 garlic clove, peeled and crushed

1 tablespoon finely chopped fresh parsley

¼ cup olive oil

1 pound redfish fillets

1½ tablespoons capers

2 anchovy fillets

1 dried red chili pepper, crumbled

Salt and freshly ground black pepper to taste

1 cup dry white wine

In this recipe, redfish, also called ocean perch, is cooked with a soffritto of onion, garlic, and parsley and finished in a spicy white wine sauce.

serves 2 to 4

1. Sauté the onion, garlic, and parsley in the olive oil over medium heat for 5 minutes, stirring often.

2. Add the fish, capers, anchovies, chili pepper, and salt and pepper. Add ⅓ cup of the wine, and increase the heat to medium high. Cook until the wine has almost evaporated. Add another ⅓ cup wine and cook until it has evaporated, carefully turning the fish a few times. Pour in the remaining ⅓ cup wine and cook until the sauce has reduced and thickened, about 20 minutes total cooking time. Remove the fish to a platter and pour the sauce over it. Serve immediately.

baked white fish gratinate

6 tablespoons olive oil

1 garlic clove, peeled and very finely chopped

8 anchovy fillets

1 pound boneless white fish steaks or fillets, about ½ inch thick

¼ cup bread crumbs

½ cup finely chopped fresh parsley

Salt and freshly ground black pepper to taste

2 to 4 lemon wedges or red pepper oil (see page 19)

This is a quick and simple version of a traditional baked hake dish from Palermo, Sicily. Almost any white fish—cod, halibut, hake, bass, pollack, catfish, turbot, monkfish, haddock—can be used. The fish will have a beautiful golden crust that you can moisten with a squirt of lemon juice or a splash of red pepper oil.

serves 2 to 4

1. Preheat the oven to 425°F.

2. In a small pan, heat 3 tablespoons of the olive oil over medium heat. Sauté the garlic for 1 minute. Add the anchovies and stir until they "melt," about 1 minute. Set aside.

3. Arrange the fish in an oiled baking dish. Sprinkle half the bread crumbs and half the parsley over the fish, and season with salt and pepper. Pour the anchovy oil over the fish and cover with the remaining bread crumbs and parsley. Drizzle the remaining 3 tablespoons olive oil over the fish.

4. Bake for 20 minutes. Remove with a spatula to a serving platter, and serve with lemon wedges or red pepper oil.

monkfish nuggets

Pure olive oil for deep-
frying

1 pound monkfish fillet,
cut in 1-inch cubes

Flour for dredging

2 large eggs, beaten

1¼ cups bread crumbs

Salt to taste

Lemon wedges

If I call deep-fried bread crumb–coated food "nuggets," my kids are guaranteed to eat it. When my daughter Dyala was three, I told her we were going to have monkfish nuggets. To this day she calls them monkey nuggets. The firmness of the monkfish makes for perfectly mouth-watering golden morsels. (To deep-fry quickly and with as little hassle as possible, see page 4.)

serves 2 to 4

1. Preheat the oven to warm (150°F to 200°F). In a large heavy pot or a deep fryer, heat the oil to 370°F.

2. Meanwhile, dredge the monkfish in the flour, shaking off the excess. Dip the fish in the eggs and then in the bread crumbs, shaking off excess crumbs.

3. Deep-fry the fish nuggets, in batches, for 2 to 2½ minutes, or until golden brown. Place on paper towels to drain, and lightly salt the fish. Then transfer the fried fish to the oven to keep warm while you continue frying. Serve immediately, with lemon wedges.

mussel and tomato salad

16 green beans, trimmed and cut into ½-inch pieces

2 pounds mussels, debearded and rinsed

⅓ cup extra virgin olive oil

Juice of 1 lemon

1 garlic clove, peeled and finely chopped

Salt to taste

10 ripe but firm cherry tomatoes, halved

½ teaspoon freshly ground black pepper

2 hard-boiled large eggs

4 anchovy fillets (optional)

Cultivated mussels are sold today already cleaned, for ease of preparation. This salad can stand alone, but it's also good with a simple pasta or grilled meat.

serves 4

1. In a saucepan of boiling water, cook the green beans until crisp-tender; drain.

2. In a steamer pot or a large pot, steam the mussels with about ½ inch of water just until they open, about 5 minutes. Discard any mussels that don't open.

3. Meanwhile, make the dressing by mixing together the olive oil, lemon juice, garlic, and salt.

4. Place the tomatoes on a serving platter. Remove all but 8 of the mussels from their shells and scatter them over the tomatoes, tossing a bit. Scatter the green beans around the tomatoes. Sprinkle with the black pepper and pour on half of the dressing.

5. Shell the hard-boiled eggs and quarter them lengthwise. Arrange decoratively around the edge of the platter. Arrange the remaining mussels around the platter. Place the anchovies, if desired, in the center of the salad, making two "Xs," and pour the remaining dressing on top. Serve immediately, or set aside at room temperature for up to 1 hour; do not refrigerate.

steamed mussels

17 pounds cleaned
    mussels

Bunch of fresh parsley,
    leaves removed and
    chopped

8 garlic cloves, peeled
    and finely chopped

1 cup olive oil

Freshly ground black
    pepper to taste
    (optional)

½ teaspoon red chili
    pepper flakes
    (optional)

Lemon wedges (optional)

You may never have ten people drop in on you unexpectedly. But if you do (or if you love mussels)—and your fishmonger has a lot of cleaned mussels on hand—then this recipe is ideal. Serve with lots of crusty Italian bread to soak up the broth.

serves 10

1. Dunk the cleaned mussels in a sink filled with cold water to wash them once more. Put the mussels into two large pots. Toss half the parsley and garlic into each pot. Pour the olive oil over the mussels. Add the black pepper and chili pepper flakes, if using.

2. Place the pots over high heat, partially cover, and heat until steam begins to rise. Stir the mussels with a long wooden spoon so they steam evenly, and cook just until they open. Discard any mussels that have not opened.

3. Pour some of the mussel liquid into dipping bowls. Serve the mussels in their pots, with lemon wedges if desired. Don't forget to place two big bowls on the table for the empty shells.

Note: Three pounds of mussels can serve 2 people. Use the leaves from 4 parsley sprigs, 2 garlic cloves, about 3 tablespoons oil, and a pinch of chili pepper flakes. In the summertime, this is a fun and messy eating experience, so don't bother with utensils (wash up afterwards).

sesame fried oysters

Pure olive oil for deep-frying

¾ cup bread crumbs

½ cup flour

¼ cup sesame seeds

1 tablespoon salt

½ teaspoon freshly ground black pepper

12 shucked oysters

Most fishmongers sell shucked oysters, making this preparation ideal for a quick dinner or snack.

serves 2 (or 4 as an appetizer)

1. In a large heavy pot or a deep fryer, heat the oil to 370°F.

2. Meanwhile, mix together all the remaining ingredients except the oysters.

3. Roll the oysters in the seasoning mix, coating them on all sides. Deep-fry for 3 minutes, or until crispy and golden. Drain on paper towels and serve hot.

Note: To serve this dish as an appetizer for company, shuck the oysters yourself and save 12 shell halves. Scrub them well, and place the fried oysters in them.

garlic and parsley shrimp

⅓ cup olive oil

1 pound shrimp, peeled

3 garlic cloves, peeled
and finely chopped

¼ cup finely chopped
fresh parsley

½ teaspoon red chili
pepper flakes

Salt and freshly ground
black pepper to taste

Peeling a pound of shrimp may take about ten to fifteen minutes—but remember that they cook in a fraction of that time. This piquant sauté of shrimp with abundant garlic and parsley can be served over pasta or with rice.

serves 2 to 4

1. In a large sauté pan, heat the olive oil over medium heat. Add the shrimp, garlic, parsley, red pepper flakes, and salt and pepper. (Be a bit liberal with the salt.) Increase the heat to high and sauté the shrimp, shaking the pan constantly, for 3 minutes. Turn the shrimp over and sauté for another 3 minutes. Remove to a platter and serve.

breaded shrimp with garlic, lemon zest, and parsley

8 jumbo shrimp (about 1 pound), peeled

Salt to taste

2 large eggs, beaten

Bread crumbs for dredging

1 cup pure or virgin olive oil

3 garlic cloves, peeled and crushed

Zest from ½ lemon, cut into extremely fine julienne

3 tablespoons finely chopped fresh parsley

Lemon wedges

This recipe is one of my favorites for shrimp.

serves 2

1. Using a sharp paring knife, slit the shrimp from head to tail along the belly, making sure you don't cut all the way through. Open the shrimp a bit with your fingers and lay them cut side down on an oiled piece of wax paper. Salt them lightly. Cover with another sheet of oiled wax paper and pound them very gently with a mallet until they are thin.

2. Dip the shrimp in the eggs and then in the bread crumbs. Set aside. (If you have 15 minutes to spare, put the shrimp on a plate in the refrigerator to set the coating.)

3. Heat the olive oil in a large pan over medium-high heat. Add the garlic cloves and sauté just until they begin to brown. Remove them and discard. Add the shrimp and cook for about 1 minute on each side. Remove to a platter, and sprinkle the lemon zest and parsley on top. Serve with lemon wedges.

Note: If you double the recipe, cook the shrimp in two large pans, or cook them in batches; don't crowd them.

shrimp in garlic cream sauce

8 jumbo shrimp (about 1 pound), peeled

Salt to taste

Flour for dredging

4 tablespoons unsalted butter

2 tablespoons olive oil

3 tablespoons finely chopped onion

2 garlic cloves, peeled and finely chopped

¼ cup finely chopped fresh parsley

1 teaspoon freshly ground white pepper

½ cup dry white wine

1 cup heavy cream

Jumbo shrimp are the easiest to butterfly. The cream sauce is fragrant with garlic and quite rich, so serve this dish with a simple steamed vegetable.

serves 2

1. Using a sharp paring knife, slit the shrimp from head to tail along the belly, making sure you don't cut all the way through. Open the shrimp a bit with your fingers and lay them cut side down on an oiled piece of wax paper. Salt them lightly. Cover with another sheet of oiled wax paper and pound them very gently with a mallet until they are thin. Dredge the shrimp in flour, shaking off the excess.

2. In a large sauté pan, melt the butter with the olive oil. Sauté the onion, garlic, and parsley for 2 minutes over high heat, stirring constantly so the garlic doesn't burn. Add the shrimp and cook for 2 minutes, turning once. Sprinkle with the white pepper, pour in the white wine, and cook until it evaporates. Pour in the heavy cream, lower the heat to medium, and cook for 2 to 4 minutes, until the sauce has thickened a bit. Serve immediately.

sardines gratinate

16 fresh sardines (about 1 ¼ pounds), cleaned and gutted

Salt and freshly ground black pepper to taste

Bread crumbs for sprinkling

Olive oil for drizzling

Fresh sardines (or defrosted frozen sardines) are by far the best choice for this simple preparation, because of their distinctive flavor. You can make it with more commonly available whiting or smelt, and it will still be good but not as exciting. Have the fishmonger clean and gut the sardines.

serves 4

1. Preheat the oven to 425°F. Oil the bottom of a baking pan.

2. Arrange the sardines in the baking pan with their heads all pointing in the same direction. Season with salt and pepper. Sprinkle with enough bread crumbs to lightly cover the sardines, and drizzle with olive oil. Bake for 15 minutes. Serve hot.

Six

Frittate e Panini

frittatas and little sandwiches

The fastest meals are often the ones we cook without looking at a recipe. When I'm too tired or not hungry enough to cook something elaborate, I often whip up a frittata, an Italian-style omelette, or make myself a *panino,* the small Italian version of the hero sandwich.

In Italy, frittatas are made with beaten eggs cooked until set on both sides and are served flat, not folded over. I make my frittatas fluffy, cooking them without flipping them over. Sometimes I fold them over in the style of an omelette or finish them under a hot broiler. If you are making frittatas for more than two people, double or triple the recipe but cook in separate pans or in batches.

Panini are little Italian sandwiches for those on the go, or for snacking. Americans extrapolated and enlarged on these sandwiches years ago to come up with the hero, submarine, or grinder. But I always love getting little *panini* at a neighborhood cafe or even at the train station when I'm in Italy. *Tramezzini* are another variety of small Italian sandwich, made with sliced white bread rather than small rolls. The recipes in this chapter go well beyond the common sausage and pepper or veal cutlet heros found in sandwich shops here.

fresh ricotta and anchovy frittata

4 ounces ricotta,
preferably fresh

6 anchovy fillets, well
rinsed

Freshly ground black
pepper to taste

½ tablespoon unsalted
butter

1 tablespoon olive oil

1 garlic clove, peeled and
crushed

3 large eggs, beaten

I like to use lots of anchovies in this frittata, but in this recipe I've cut the amount I normally use by half. The mild flavor of ricotta goes well with the sharper anchovy taste. Remember that even after washing the salt off the anchovies they will still be salty, making additional salt unnecessary.

serves 1 to 2

1. Preheat the broiler.

2. Mash the ricotta, anchovies, and pepper together. Set aside.

3. Heat the butter and olive oil in a 10-inch ovenproof frying pan and sauté the crushed garlic until it just begins to turn light brown. Remove the garlic and discard. Pour in the beaten eggs and sprinkle the ricotta and anchovy mixture on top. Let the bottom set, then remove the pan from the heat and place under the broiler until the top sets, about 2 minutes. Serve.

artichoke frittata

3 large eggs

2 tablespoons finely
    chopped fresh
    parsley

Salt and freshly ground
    black pepper to taste

3 canned artichoke
    hearts, finely
    chopped

1 garlic clove, peeled and
    finely chopped

1 tablespoon freshly
    grated Parmesan

1 tablespoon olive oil

This frittata makes a satisfying lunch dish.

serves 1 to 2

1. In a medium bowl, beat the eggs, parsley, and salt and pepper together. Add the artichokes, garlic, and Parmesan and blend well.

2. Heat the olive oil in a 10-inch frying pan. Add the egg mixture and shake the pan while it sets, about 1 minute over medium heat. Fold over like an omelette or flip carefully with a spatula and cook for another 30 seconds. Transfer to a plate and serve immediately.

ziti and fontina frittata

3 large eggs, separated

Salt and freshly ground
black pepper to taste

1 canned artichoke heart,
chopped

2 tablespoons unsalted
butter

1 cup cooked ziti or
macaroni

1 tablespoon finely
chopped fresh
parsley

2 ounces Fontina, cut
into 3 to 4 slices

This is a great lunch frittata that uses left-over pasta, so it takes only ten minutes to prepare and cook.

serves 1 to 2

1. Preheat the broiler.

2. In a medium bowl, beat the egg yolks and salt and pepper. In another bowl, whip the egg whites until they form soft peaks. Fold the egg yolks into the whites. Fold in the artichoke.

3. Melt the butter in a 10-inch ovenproof omelette or frying pan. When the butter stops sizzling, add the egg mixture to the pan. Quickly scatter the ziti and parsley over the eggs and layer the Fontina on top. Then transfer the pan to the broiler and broil for 3 minutes, or until the cheese has melted.

4. Using a spatula, if necessary, slide the frittata onto a plate, flipping it over itself like an omelette. Serve immediately.

zucchini and olive frittata

2 tablespoons olive oil

3 tablespoons finely
chopped onion

1 large garlic clove,
peeled and finely
chopped

½ stalk celery, finely
chopped

2 small zucchini, peeled
and thinly sliced (or
use the zucchini
pulp from Baked
Stuffed Zucchini,
page 180)

4 large imported green
Sicilian (Paternò)
olives, pitted and
chopped

Salt and freshly ground
black pepper to taste

3 large eggs

¼ cup freshly grated
Parmesan

I love to make this frittata when my zucchini plant is in full production. The olives make it really terrific. Sometimes I make a second one to serve later or the next day at room temperature as an antipasto.

serves 1 to 2

1. Heat the olive oil in a 10-inch frying pan. Sauté the onion, garlic, celery, and zucchini for 5 minutes over medium-high heat, stirring frequently. Add the olives and salt and pepper, stir, and cook for 2 minutes.

2. Meanwhile, in a small bowl, beat the eggs, and stir in the Parmesan.

3. Pour the eggs into the pan. Cook until the bottom is set, about 1 minute, then flip over carefully with a spatula. Cook for another minute and serve.

Note: You can also finish the frittata under a broiler rather than flipping it over.

gorgonzola, olive, and tomato frittata

2 tablespoons olive oil

3 large eggs

3 tablespoons freshly
grated Parmesan

1 small ripe plum tomato,
finely chopped

6 imported black olives,
pitted and chopped

2 ounces Gorgonzola,
crumbled

Salt and freshly ground
black pepper to taste

1 tablespoon finely
chopped fresh
parsley

Gorgonzola, a pungent cheese, is an ideal contrast to the relatively mild taste of eggs. The tomato and parsley make for a colorful and attractive dish.

serves 1 to 2

1. Preheat the broiler.

2. Heat the olive oil in a 10-inch ovenproof omelette pan or a frying pan over medium-high heat. In a medium bowl, beat the eggs and beat in the Parmesan. Then pour the eggs into the pan. Sprinkle the tomato, olives, Gorgonzola, and salt and pepper on top. Transfer the pan to the broiler and broil until the top sets and the cheese melts, about 3 minutes.

3. Sprinkle the parsley on top of the frittata. Slide it onto a plate and serve.

mozzarella, tomato, and basil frittata

3 large eggs

Salt and freshly ground
    black pepper to taste

2 tablespoons butter

1 ripe plum tomato,
    thinly sliced

5 fresh basil leaves,
    finely chopped

3 ounces fresh
    mozzarella, thinly
    sliced

4 anchovy fillets,
    chopped

This absolutely heavenly frittata is one of my favorites. The secret ingredient is the anchovies, which give it a wonderfully special taste. I usually make it so the eggs remain a bit soft.

serves 1 to 2

1. Preheat the broiler.

2. Beat the eggs and lightly season with salt and pepper.

3. Melt the butter in a 10-inch ovenproof omelette or frying pan. When the butter stops bubbling, pour in the eggs. Layer the tomato, basil, mozzarella, and anchovies on top. Cook until the bottom has set, about 1 minute, then transfer to the broiler. Broil until the top has set and the cheese has melted, 1 to 2 minutes. Pour off any excess water from the mozzarella. Slide the frittata onto a warm plate and serve.

pancetta and parmesan frittata

1 tablespoon unsalted
butter

2 ounces pancetta (in 1
piece), sliced into
strips

3 large eggs, beaten well

⅓ cup freshly grated
Parmesan

2 tablespoons finely
chopped fresh
parsley

Freshly ground black
pepper to taste

Pancetta is cured Italian bacon with a taste somewhere between that of regular bacon and prosciutto. It can be eaten raw, because of the curing process, but it has a delicious crisp taste when cooked, further enhanced by the fresh Parmesan in this frittata.

serves 1 to 2

1. Preheat the broiler

2. In a 10-inch ovenproof omelette pan or frying pan, melt the butter with the pancetta over medium heat. Cook, stirring, for about 3 minutes. Then arrange the pancetta evenly over the bottom of the pan and carefully pour in the eggs. Sprinkle the cheese, parsley, and pepper on top.

3. Transfer to the broiler and broil until the top sets, about 1 to 2 minutes. Slide the frittata onto a plate, flipping one half over the other, and serve.

frittata con formaggio

2 tablespoons olive oil

1 garlic clove, peeled and crushed

3 large eggs, beaten

Salt and freshly ground black pepper to taste

1 ounce fresh mozzarella, sliced into 4 pieces

1 ounce fresh ricotta, sliced into 4 pieces (or 4 dollops of commercial ricotta)

1 ounce Fontina, sliced into 4 pieces

4 anchovy fillets (optional)

2 tablespoons finely chopped fresh parsley

Cheese and eggs is one of my favorite combinations. If you use fresh cheeses in this dish, your frittata may be slightly watery; if you prefer a drier frittata, use commercial mozzarella and ricotta.

serves 1 to 2

1. Preheat the broiler.

2. In a 10-inch ovenproof omelette pan or frying pan, heat the olive oil and very lightly brown the garlic clove. Remove and discard the garlic. Pour in the eggs and salt and pepper. Layer the cheeses on top, along with the anchovies, if using, and sprinkle with the parsley.

3. Transfer the pan to the broiler and broil until the edges of the frittata are light brown and the cheeses have melted, about 3 minutes. Serve.

eggs with fish roe

1 tablespoon olive oil

1 garlic clove, peeled and crushed

3 large eggs

1 to 2 ounces fish roe, chopped if fresh

1 tablespoon finely chopped fresh parsley

Salt and freshly ground black pepper to taste

Freshly grated Pecorino

Many fishmongers do not save, let alone sell, the eggs they find when filleting whole fish. This is a great shame since fish roe (call it caviar, if you prefer) has a delicious taste that can dress up a simple egg preparation. Ask the fishmonger to set aside roe for you; cod, bluefish, haddock, dab, and red snapper roe are especially good. Use the roe the same day you purchase it, or freeze it. If you are unable to find fresh fish roe, use the salmon roe available in supermarkets, although the taste will be entirely different.

serves 1 to 2

1. In a sauté pan, heat the olive oil over medium-low heat. Cook the garlic clove until it just begins to turn light brown. Remove and discard the garlic.

2. Meanwhile, in a bowl, beat the eggs, roe, parsley, and salt and pepper together.

3. Add the eggs to the pan and shake the pan until the mixture sets, about 1 minute. Fold over like an omelette and cook for another 30 seconds. The inside should still be creamy. Immediately transfer to a plate and sprinkle with Pecorino.

Note: You can double the recipe for more than two people, but cook in two pans.

pizza frittata

1½ tablespoons unsalted
    butter

1 tablespoon olive oil

4 large eggs

½ teaspoon salt

4 thin slices ripe tomato

6 imported black olives,
    pitted and chopped

6 thin slices Fontina

1 tablespoon finely
    chopped fresh
    parsley

Letting the sides of this beautiful frittata puff up under the broiler makes it look like a pizza with a golden crust. It is a perfect light supper dish.

serves 2

1. Preheat the broiler

2. In a 10-inch ovenproof omelette pan or frying pan, heat the butter and olive oil until the butter just begins to brown. Meanwhile, beat the eggs with the salt.

3. Pour the eggs into the pan. Quickly arrange the tomato slices on top, and then sprinkle the olives over them. Cover with the Fontina and sprinkle on the parsley.

4. Transfer to the broiler and broil until the top is set and lightly speckled with brown and the edges have puffed up. Serve immediately.

prosciutto, avocado, and tomato panini

4 soft rolls

Extra virgin olive oil for
drizzling

4 to 6 ounces prosciutto
di Parma, thinly
sliced

3 ripe plum tomatoes,
sliced

1 small ripe avocado,
stoned and very
thinly sliced

4 fresh basil leaves,
chopped

Salt and freshly ground
black pepper to taste

Slice the avocado quite thin—otherwise the slices will slip out when you bite down.

serves 4

1. Slice the rolls open, and, drizzle olive oil over the insides. Layer the prosciutto, tomatoes, and avocado on the bottoms of the rolls. Sprinkle with the basil, and then lightly with salt and pepper. Put the tops on and press down gently.

porchetta and mozzarella panini

4 soft rolls

Extra virgin olive oil for
drizzling

Freshly ground black
pepper to taste

4 to 6 ounces porchetta,
thinly sliced

6 ounces fresh
mozzarella, sliced

Porchetta is an Italian-style roast pork available in Italian delicatessens.

serves 4

1. Slice open the rolls. Drizzle the insides with olive oil. Sprinkle with pepper. Layer the porchetta and mozzarella on the bottoms of the rolls. Put on the tops and press down gently.

taleggio and tomato panini

4 soft rolls

Red pepper olive oil (see
    page 19) or extra
    virgin olive oil for
    drizzling

4 ounces Taleggio, cut
    into 8 slices

4 ripe plum tomatoes,
    sliced

Salt and freshly ground
    black pepper to taste

Taleggio is a mild semisoft whole cow's milk cheese from the Lombardy region of Italy, perfect with tomatoes. It is most flavorful at room temperature.

serves 4

1. Slice open the rolls. Drizzle pepper oil over the bottoms of the rolls. Top with the cheese and then the tomatoes. Sprinkle with salt and pepper. Put the tops on and press down gently.

prosciutto and hearts of palm panini

4 soft rolls

Mayonnaise for
    spreading

Freshly ground black
    pepper to taste

4 ripe plum tomatoes,
    thinly sliced

4 ounces hearts of palm
    packed in water,
    sliced lengthwise

4 to 6 ounces prosciutto
    di Parma, thinly
    sliced

Hearts of palm are usually sold canned in water, commonly found in the Hispanic products section of supermarkets. They are tender and mild-tasting.

serves 4

1. Slice open the rolls. Spread with mayonnaise, and sprinkle with pepper. Layer the tomatoes, hearts of palm, and prosciutto on the bottoms of the rolls. Put the tops on and press down gently.

olives and mozzarella panini

4 soft rolls

Extra virgin olive oil for drizzling

Freshly ground black pepper to taste

½ cup chopped pitted large imported Sicilian (Paternò) green olives

6 ounces fresh mozzarella, sliced

The tangy olives and the mild mozzarella provide a nice contrast to one another.

serves 4

1. Slice open the rolls. Drizzle the insides with olive oil. Sprinkle with pepper. Sprinkle the olives over the bottoms of the rolls and layer the mozzarella on top. Put the tops on and press down gently.

shrimp and sliced egg panini

4 soft rolls

Mayonaise for spreading

½ pound peeled cooked medium shrimp

Salt and freshly ground black pepper to taste

2 to 3 hard-boiled eggs, sliced

Near the apartment I once rented in Venice was a café, where I would treat myself every morning to this marvelous panino, along with a cappucino. Buy cooked shrimp to save time.

serves 4

1. Slice open the rolls, and spread with mayonnaise. Lay the shrimp on the bottoms of the rolls and sprinkle with salt and pepper. Cover with the eggs and then the tops of the rolls. Press down gently.

parmesan, olive, and anchovy panini

4 soft rolls

Extra virgin olive oil for drizzling

About 2 ounces shavings fresh Parmesan

½ cup chopped pitted large imported Sicilian (Paternò) green olives

8 anchovy fillets

For this panino *you need a large chunk of Parmesan so you can shave off thin pieces with a sharp knife or the slicing side of a cheese grater.*

serves 4

1. Slice open the rolls. Drizzle the olive oil over the insides. Layer the Parmesan shavings on the bottoms of the rolls, and cover with the olives and anchovy fillets. Put the tops on and press down gently.

asparagus and anchovy panini

4 soft rolls

Mayonnaise for spreading

8 ounces canned asparagus, drained

8 to 16 anchovy fillets (to taste)

Canned asparagus is very tender and perfect for sandwiches.

serves 4

1. Slice open the rolls, and spread with mayonnaise. Lay the asparagus on the bottoms and top with the anchovy fillets. Put the tops on and press down gently.

crab and asparagus panini

4 soft rolls

Mayonnaise for
    spreading

6 to 8 ounces cooked
    crabmeat, picked
    over for shells and
    cartilage

6 ounces canned
    asparagus, drained

This is one of my favorite panini.

serves 4

1. Slice open the rolls, and spread with mayonnaise. Place the crab and then the asparagus on the bottoms of the rolls. Put the tops on and press down gently.

fresh fig, prosciutto, and mozzarella panini

4 soft rolls

Extra virgin olive oil for
    drizzling

4 fresh figs, sliced in half

4 to 6 ounces prosciutto
    di Parma, thinly
    sliced

4 ounces fresh
    mozzarella, sliced

When figs are in season in late spring, try this deliciously sweet panino, *with or without the mozzarella.*

serves 4

1. Slice open the rolls. Drizzle olive oil over the bottoms. Place the halved figs on the bottoms of the rolls and press down to flatten. Layer the prosciutto and mozzarella on top and cover with the tops of the rolls. Press down gently.

mozzarella in carrozza

½ pound fresh
    mozzarella, cut into
    8 slices

Flour for dredging

2 large eggs, beaten

Bread crumbs for
    dredging

1 cup pure olive oil

1 garlic clove, peeled

8 anchovy fillets

Extra virgin olive oil for
    drizzling (optional)

2 tablespoons finely
    chopped fresh
    parsley

This is my simplified version of the famous Neapolitan dish. I use bread crumbs instead of bread and it takes only minutes to make.

serves 4

1. Dredge the slices of mozzarella in the flour, shaking off any excess. Dip each slice in the beaten eggs and dredge in the bread crumbs. Then dip again in the eggs and dredge in the crumbs. Set aside.

2. In a large pan, heat the pure olive oil with the garlic clove over medium-high heat until the garlic begins to turn light brown. Remove and discard. Using tongs, slide the cheese into the oil. Fry for about 2 minutes, then turn over and fry for another 2 minutes, or until golden brown on both sides. (If any cheese starts to melt and escape into the oil, remove immediately.)

3. Place the mozzarella on a plate and lay an anchovy fillet on top of each piece. Drizzle some olive oil over if desired, and sprinkle with the parsley. Serve immediately.

Seven

Verdure e Contorni

vegetables and side dishes

One of the delights of Italian cooking is fresh vegetables quickly prepared in a variety of imaginative ways. The secret is to use the freshest possible ingredients: The vegetables should be young, tender, and unblemished. Green beans should snap, celery should crunch, broccoli florets should be bright green and tight, and ripe tomatoes should have taste.

I find Italian vegetable cookery so exciting and I serve vegetables so often that people ask me if I am a vegetarian. I always answer no—I'm a vegophile. I love vegetables sweet or savory, in salads or stews, as antipasti, both cooked and raw. Tiny raw fava beans can be eaten with a simple dressing of olive oil and lemon juice. Carrots can be cut into sticks and served with an olive oil– or mayonnaise-based dip or eaten plain. The same goes for celery, fennel, broccoli, and a host of other vegetables. Add just a sprinkle of salt—it's amazing how the "simpler the better" dictum is true for vegetables.

The recipes in this chapter are for fresh vegetable dishes that can be cooked quickly but are a little more involved than the fast and simple way I most often cook vegetables—steamed and served with a light drizzle of olive oil. Some of these dishes could be served as meals in themselves, others are accompaniments to main courses, but all are easy to put together.

celery, roasted red pepper, and olive salad

1 roasted red bell pepper
(see page 19),
coarsely chopped

3 stalks celery, washed,
trimmed, and sliced
diagonally into ½-
inch pieces

¼ pound Bel Paese,
diced (optional)

4 anchovy fillets,
chopped (optional)

12 large imported Sicilian
(Paternò) green
olives, pitted

3 tablespoons extra
virgin olive oil

Freshly ground black
pepper to taste
(optional)

This is a fast salad, full of color—a natural with Grilled Filet Mignon with Pancetta and Rosemary (page 89).

serves 2

1. Place the red bell pepper, celery, cheese, if using, anchovies, if using, and olives in a large bowl. Toss, add the olive oil and black pepper, if using, and toss again. Serve at room temperature.

fennel, onion, tomato, and green olive salad

1 large fennel bulb (about
    1½ pounds),
    trimmed and
    chopped

1 small onion, peeled and
    chopped

4 ripe plum tomatoes,
    quartered and
    seeded

12 large imported Sicilian
    (Paternò) green
    olives, pitted

1 garlic clove, peeled and
    finely chopped

Salt and freshly ground
    black pepper to taste

Extra virgin olive oil to
    taste

8 fresh mint leaves,
    finely chopped

The crunch of fresh raw fennel makes a nice companion for grilled food, such as Furious Chicken (page 104).

serves 4 to 6

1. In a large bowl, mix all the ingredients together, and toss well. Serve at room temperature.

boston lettuce with herb vinaigrette

½ cup extra virgin olive
  oil

2 tablespoons balsamic
  vinegar

2 garlic cloves, peeled
  and mashed

4 anchovy fillets,
  chopped

Finely chopped fresh
  basil, oregano, or
  thyme to taste

Salt and freshly ground
  black pepper to taste

2 heads Boston lettuce,
  washed, dried, and
  torn into bite-sized
  pieces

8 cherry tomatoes,
  halved, or 4 plum
  tomatoes, quartered
  (optional)

I serve this basic salad with red meat or rich dishes such as Veal with Hazelnuts (page 93). If you are serving a dish with sweet-and-sour flavors, you might want to replace the lettuce with dandelion, which makes for a bitter contrast.

serves 4

1. Prepare the vinaigrette by whisking together the oil, vinegar, garlic, anchovies, herb, and salt and pepper.

2. Pour the vinaigrette over the lettuce and toss. Garnish with the tomatoes.

carrots with marsala

1 tablespoon olive oil

1 pound baby carrots, scrubbed

½ cup water

2 teaspoons sugar

Salt to taste

½ cup sweet Marsala wine

Baby carrots do not need to be peeled, making this Sicilian recipe a real snap.

serves 2 to 4

1. In a frying pan, heat the olive oil. Sauté the carrots over medium-high heat for 1 minute. Pour in the water and simmer until most of it has evaporated. Sprinkle the carrots with the sugar and salt and cook, stirring, until lightly caramelized, about 1 minute.

2. Pour in the Marsala wine and continue cooking until it has nearly evaporated. Serve immediately.

green beans with pine nuts

1 pound green beans, trimmed

2 tablespoons olive oil

¼ cup pine nuts

This is about the easiest way to make green beans sparkle—in both taste and color. I often serve these with red meat.

serves 4

1. Bring a large pot of lightly salted water to a boil. Blanch the green beans for 4 minutes, drain, and cool quickly under cold running water to stop the cooking.

2. In a sauté pan, heat the olive oil. Sauté the pine nuts for 1 minute. Add the beans and cook just until the pine nuts begin to brown. Immediately remove from the heat, and serve.

green beans wrapped in prosciutto

½ lemon

Salt

½ pound green beans, trimmed

4 to 8 thin slices prosciutto di Parma

8 to 12 slivers of lemon peel

These little packages of green beans wrapped in prosciutto make an attractive appetizer or cocktail snack. Or serve as a side dish to Fettuccine with Prosciutto and Zucchini Blossoms (page 67) or with Butterflied Pork Tenderloin with Nut Sauce (page 97).

serves 2 to 4

1. Fill a small pot with water, add the lemon half and a little salt, and bring to a boil. Add the green beans, and cook for about 8 minutes; the green beans should still be crunchy. Drain, and let cool for 2 minutes.

2. Lay several green beans across one end of a slice of prosciutto and roll the prosciutto up. Repeat with the remaining beans and prosciutto and arrange on a serving platter. With the lemon peel slivers, make an "X" on each roll-up, and serve.

spinach sautéed in garlic and olive oil

1¼ pounds (20 ounces) fresh spinach, washed and trimmed

2 garlic cloves, peeled and very finely chopped

¼ cup extra virgin olive oil

Salt and freshly ground black pepper to taste

Sautéed spinach is the height of simplicity but extraordinary in taste considering how few ingredients are involved. Dunk the spinach twice in a large pot of cold water and swish it around to remove any sand, and then remove the heavier stems.

serves 4

1. Place the spinach in a large pot and steam over gentle heat for 2 minutes, or until wilted. Drain well, pressing out as much excess water as you can with the back of a wooden spoon.

2. In a frying pan, sauté the garlic in the olive oil over low heat for 3 minutes. Add the spinach and mix well. Cook for 8 to 10 minutes. Season with salt and pepper, and serve.

sautéed red swiss chard

1¼ pounds red Swiss chard (see Note)

¼ cup olive oil

4 garlic cloves, peeled and finely chopped

Salt and freshly ground black pepper to taste

4 tablespoons unsalted butter

Swiss chard is a member of the beet family. It can be cooked like spinach but has a more pronounced flavor. White Swiss chard is more common, but red Swiss chard, with its brilliant blood-red stalks, sautéed in butter, olive oil and an abundant amount of garlic, is both striking and delectable.

serves 4

1. Wash the Swiss chard by dunking and swishing it in several changes of cold water. Rip it into smaller pieces, discarding the harder parts of the stalks. Remove as much water as possible from the chard in a salad spinner.

2. Place the chard in a large pot and steam over medium heat until it wilts, tossing often so it doesn't burn. Drain well.

3. In a large pot, heat the olive oil with the garlic over medium heat for 2 minutes. Add the Swiss chard and salt and pepper, cover, and cook for 2 to 3 minutes. Stir in the butter and cook until the butter has melted and the chard is cooked to your taste. Serve.

Note: This recipe can also be made with spinach.

sweet-and-sour celery

2 tablespoons sugar

¼ cup balsamic vinegar

½ cup olive oil

4 cups celery sliced on the diagonal

1 garlic clove, peeled and finely chopped

1½ tablespoons finely chopped fresh mint

This dish is best served at room temperature or warm. As it takes only about fifteen minutes from start to finish, you should have time to wait for it to cool. It can also be made ahead of time and reheated slightly.

serves 2 to 4

1. Dissolve the sugar in the vinegar.

2. Pour the olive oil into a deep pot and heat over high heat until smoking hot. Add the celery and garlic and cook, stirring frequently, for about 7 minutes. Add the vinegar and sugar and stir constantly until the vinegar has nearly evaporated. Immediately remove from the heat, stir in 1 tablespoon of the mint, and transfer to a serving platter. Garnish with the remaining ½ tablespoon mint.

sweet-and-sour cauliflower and mushrooms

¾ pound cauliflower, separated into florets

3 tablespoons olive oil

¾ pound mushrooms, cleaned and sliced

8 scallions, white part only, chopped

1 celery heart or 1 large stalk, chopped

⅓ cup dry white wine

1 tablespoon pine nuts

4 large imported Sicilian (Paternò) green olives, pitted and chopped

1 tablespoon red wine vinegar

1 tablespoon sugar

⅛ teaspoon red chili pepper flakes

Salt and freshly ground black pepper to taste

This vibrantly flavored dish is substantial enough to be served in larger portions as a main course.

serves 4

1. Bring a pot of lightly salted water to a boil. Cook the cauliflower for 8 minutes, or until crisp-tender; drain.

2. Meanwhile, in a large pan, heat the olive oil. Sauté the mushrooms, scallions, and celery over high heat for 4 minutes, stirring constantly. Add the wine and cook for 4 minutes. Add the pine nuts, olives, vinegar, sugar, red pepper flakes, and salt and pepper and cook for 2 minutes, stirring constantly. Add the cauliflower and stir well. Cover, lower the heat to medium low, and cook for 15 minutes until the cauliflower is tender. Serve.

sweet-and-sour squash with mint

1 tablespoon sugar

¼ cup red wine vinegar

⅓ cup olive oil

1 pound winter squash, peeled and cut into ¼-inch slices

3 garlic cloves, peeled and finely chopped

Salt and freshly ground black pepper to taste

½ cup loosely packed fresh mint leaves, finely chopped

Here's a delicious way to flavor winter squash. This dish can be served at room temperature or hot. Pumpkin, Hubbard, acorn, and butternut squash all work well in this recipe.

serves 4

1. Dissolve the sugar in the wine vinegar.

2. In a large skillet, heat the olive oil over medium heat. Add the squash and garlic and cook for 5 minutes.

3. Turn the squash carefully, using a spatula, and sprinkle with salt and pepper. Add the wine vinegar and sugar and cook until it has almost evaporated. Sprinkle the mint over the squash, and cook for 1 more minute. Serve, or let cool to room temperature.

mixed vegetable sauté

6 ounces green beans, trimmed and snapped into 1-inch lengths

6 ounces broccoli, separated into florets

⅓ cup olive oil

1 stalk celery, finely chopped

2 garlic cloves, peeled and finely chopped

1 small green bell pepper, cored, seeded, and thinly sliced

4 anchovy fillets

5 large imported Sicilian (Paternò) green olives, pitted and chopped

3 tablespoons fresh oregano leaves

Salt and freshly ground black pepper to taste

1 tablespoon tomato paste dissolved in ½ cup hot water

This dish is a great way to use up small amounts of fresh vegetables. It is good tossed with penne or served with grilled meats, such as Grilled Skewers of Sausage, Orange, and Bay Leaf (page 99).

serves 2 to 4

1. Bring a large pot of lightly salted water to a boil. Blanch the green beans and broccoli in the water for 3 minutes; drain. Set aside.

2. In a large frying pan, heat the olive oil. Sauté the celery, garlic, and green pepper over medium-high heat for 4 minutes, stirring often. Add the anchovies, olives, and oregano and stir for a minute or so until the anchovies have "melted." Add the green beans, broccoli, and salt and pepper and cook, stirring, for 2 to 3 minutes. Pour in the diluted tomato paste, stir, and cook for 4 minutes. Transfer to a serving platter and let rest for 10 minutes before serving.

tomato stuffed with prosciutto, figs, and mint

10 small ripe plum
  tomatoes, halved
  lengthwise

Salt to taste

5 thin slices prosciutto di
  Parma (about ¼
  pound), cut into
  quarters

10 ripe figs, cut in half

5 tablespoons finely
  chopped fresh mint

There is no cooking involved in this recipe. These tomatoes are an unusual accompaniment to grilled foods, or serve them as an appetizer.

serves 4

1. Using a teaspoon, scoop out the seeds and pulp from the tomatoes. Lightly salt the tomatoes. Stuff a piece of prosciutto into each tomato half.

2. Using a teaspoon, scoop out the flesh from the figs, and stuff into the tomato halves; discard the fig skins. Sprinkle the mint on top and serve. (Do not refrigerate.)

red peppers with capers, anchovies, and marjoram

4 red bell peppers, cored, seeded, and cut lengthwise into ½-inch strips

2 garlic cloves, peeled and sliced crosswise

2 tablespoons olive oil

1 tablespoon capers

5 anchovy fillets

1 tablespoon fresh marjoram leaves or ½ teaspoon dried

Salt to taste (optional)

The aromatic ingredients make this dish a beautiful partner for chicken, but the peppers could also be served on toast points for an appetizing crostini or as a topping for spaghetti.

serves 4

1 . Place the red peppers, garlic, and oil in a sauté pan and cook over medium heat for 5 minutes, stirring frequently. Add the capers, anchovy fillets, and marjoram. Taste and add salt if necessary. Cook for 20 minutes, stirring occasionally. Add a few tablespoons of water if the pan seems dry. Serve warm.

oven-roasted tomatoes with provolone, pine nuts, and oregano

¼ cup olive oil

2 large ripe tomatoes, sliced about ⅜ inch thick (8 slices)

⅔ cup bread crumbs

1 to 2 garlic cloves, peeled and finely chopped

1 tablespoon finely chopped fresh basil

2 teaspoons dried oregano

2 teaspoons pine nuts

Salt and freshly ground black pepper to taste

8 2-inch by 2-inch slices provolone (about ⅟₁₆ inch thick)

Large ripe but firm tomatoes are perfect for this dish. Tomato slices are covered with a bread crumb, garlic, and oregano mixture and quickly roasted.

serves 2 to 4

1. Preheat the oven to 425°F. Oil a 9-inch by 12-inch baking pan with 1 tablespoon of the olive oil.

2. Arrange the tomatoes in the baking pan.

3. In a small pan, heat the remaining 3 tablespoons olive oil over medium heat. Add the bread crumbs, garlic, basil, oregano, pine nuts, and salt and pepper, and sauté for 3 minutes. Remove from the heat.

4. Spoon about a tablespoon of the bread crumb mixture over each slice of tomato. Cover each tomato slice with a slice of cheese. Roast for 15 minutes. Serve.

broiled tomatoes with fontina

6 small plum tomatoes,
halved lengthwise

Salt and freshly ground
black pepper to taste

¼ to ½ teaspoon dried
oregano

Olive oil for drizzling

12 slices Fontina Val
d'Aosta, cut the
same size as the
tomato halves (about
⅛ inch thick)

Fresh oregano leaves

*Use only ripe but firm plum tomatoes. They
have to be salted just right, with just enough
oregano. You may like more pepper or more
oregano—season according to your own
taste.*

serves 4

1. Preheat the broiler.

2. Using a teaspoon, scoop out the seeds
and pulp from the tomatoes. Arrange the
halves on a lightly oiled broiling tray or pan.
Sprinkle with salt and pepper, dried oregano, and a drizzle of olive oil. Place a piece
of cheese on top of each tomato half.

3. Broil for 8 to 10 minutes, until the
cheese is melted. Garnish with fresh oregano leaves and serve.

Note: You could serve these tomatoes on
top of Garlic Bread (page 11), for a summery
bruschetta.

roasted red peppers stuffed with mozzarella and prosciutto

½ pound fresh
    mozzarella

6 thin slices prosciutto di
    Parma (about ¼
    pound), cut in half

3 large roasted red
    peppers, cut
    lengthwise into
    quarters

5 large fresh basil leaves,
    chopped

Extra virgin olive oil for
    drizzling

Freshly ground black
    pepper to taste

The excellent roasted red peppers available in Italian groceries make this side dish or antipasto an easy five-minute preparation.

serves 2 to 4

1. Slice the mozzarella into 12 rectangles about 3 inches by ½ inch. Place each piece of cheese on a piece of prosciutto and roll up. Stuff a wrapped cheese rectangle inside each roasted pepper quarter.

2. Arrange attractively on a platter. Sprinkle the basil over all. Drizzle the olive oil over the prosciutto, add a sprinkling of pepper, and serve.

asparagus with hot pepper dressing

10 ounces thin
asparagus, trimmed

⅔ cup finely chopped
fresh parsley

2 garlic cloves, peeled
and finely chopped

½ teaspoon red chili
pepper flakes or ½
jalapeño pepper,
finely chopped, or
more to taste

Salt and freshly ground
black pepper to taste

Cooks in the Abruzzi region of central Italy are fond of using red chili peppers in preparations called alla diavolo, *"like the devil." You could also use a nontraditional jalapeño pepper in this spicy sauce.*

serves 4

1. Bring about an inch of lightly salted water to a boil in a large frying pan. Cook the asparagus until it is to your liking.

2. Meanwhile, prepare the dressing by mixing the parsley, garlic, chili pepper flakes or jalapeño, and salt and pepper. Taste and adjust the seasonings if necessary.

3. Drain the asparagus. Spoon the dressing over, and serve.

asparagus with pistachios

10 ounces thin
    asparagus, trimmed

2 tablespoons pistachio
    nuts

2 tablespoons olive oil

1 garlic clove, peeled and
    finely chopped

3 anchovy fillets

Salt and freshly ground
    black pepper to taste

I often serve cold asparagus with mayonnaise or hollandaise, but the unusual flavors of pistachio and anchovy in this recipe give the spears a new twist.

serves 4

1. Bring about an inch of water to a boil in a frying pan. Cook the asparagus until it is to your liking. Drain, and cool under cold running water.

2. Meanwhile, in a small frying pan, sauté the pistachios in 1 tablespoon of the oil for 3 minutes. Set aside. Cut the asparagus into 1-inch lengths, or leave it whole, as you prefer. Heat the remaining 1 tablespoon olive oil in a sauté pan. Add the asparagus, garlic, and anchovies and sauté for about 3 minutes. Season with salt and pepper. Sprinkle the pistachios on top of the asparagus, and serve.

broccoli with olives and lemon zest

1 garlic clove, peeled and crushed

½ cup olive oil

3 large stalks broccoli

½ cup imported oil-cured black olives (pitted or unpitted)

½ teaspoon red chili pepper flakes

Grated zest of ½ lemon

Salt and freshly ground black pepper to taste

What a beautiful dish! The brilliant green of broccoli, the pitch black of the olives, and the sunny flecks of lemon zest make for a very appetizing presentation.

serves 4

1. Combine the garlic and olive oil. Set aside.

2. Steam the broccoli until crisp-tender. Let cool, then slice the stalks and separate the florets.

3. Combine the broccoli, olives, red pepper flakes, lemon zest, oil and garlic, and salt and pepper. Serve at room temperature.

zucchini with anchovies, lemon, and mint

1 small onion, peeled and
    finely chopped

1 garlic clove, peeled and
    finely chopped

⅓ cup olive oil

4 anchovy fillets

Juice of ½ lemon

3 zucchini, sliced
    diagonally

Salt and freshly ground
    black pepper to taste

2 tablespoons finely
    chopped fresh mint
    leaves.

The solitary zucchini plant in my garden produces enough zucchini to feed a family of ten. Here zucchini is sautéed with a deliciously tangy combination of lemon, anchovy, and mint.

serves 4

1. In a large skillet, sauté the onion and garlic in the olive oil over medium-high heat for 4 to 5 minutes, stirring often. Add the anchovies and lemon juice and sauté until the anchovies "melt," 1 to 2 minutes. Add the zucchini and salt and pepper and cook, stirring often, for 12 to 15 minutes, or until tender.

2. Toss in the mint, and serve.

zucchini with oregano and garlic

¼ cup olive oil

3 zucchini, sliced into ⅜-inch-thick rounds

Salt and freshly ground black pepper to taste

2 garlic cloves, peeled and finely chopped

3 tablespoons fresh oregano leaves or 1 teaspoon dried

Here's another trusty recipe for a dish I love to eat with crusty Italian bread—or on top of pasta.

serves 2 to 4

1. In a large frying pan, heat the olive oil over high heat for 2 minutes. Turn the heat down to medium, add the zucchini and salt and pepper, and sauté for 3 minutes, stirring to coat the zucchini with oil. Stir in the garlic and oregano, and cook for 10 minutes. Serve.

zucchini with tomatoes

2 tablespoons olive oil

1 medium onion, peeled and thinly sliced

2 garlic cloves, peeled and finely chopped

2 zucchini, thinly sliced

1 plum tomato, chopped

1 tablespoon finely chopped fresh basil

Salt and freshly ground black pepper to taste

This quick zucchini dish is delicious at room temperature or with Sauté of Sausage, Mushrooms, and Artichokes (page 100).

serves 2

1. Heat the olive oil in a medium frying pan. Sauté the onion and garlic over medium-high heat for 5 minutes. Add the zucchini, tomato, basil, and salt and pepper, and cook, stirring and turning the zucchini occasionally, for 10 to 15 minutes. Serve warm or at room temperature.

Vegetables and side dishes **179**

baked stuffed zucchini

2 medium to large
zucchini, washed

Salt to taste

½ cup fresh bread
crumbs

1 teaspoon dried
currants

1 teaspoon pine nuts

1 teaspoon finely
chopped onion

2 tablespoons finely
chopped fresh
parsley

1 small garlic clove,
peeled and finely
chopped

1 tablespoon freshly
grated Pecorino

Freshly ground black
pepper to taste

Olive oil for drizzling

2 ounces mozzarella,
sliced

¼ cup tomato sauce (or
1 tablespoon tomato
paste mixed with 3
tablespoons water)

When you find yourself with zucchini that have grown a little too big, just hollow out the squash like canoes and stuff them with bread crumbs, currants, and pine nuts. Stuffed zucchini freezes well, and the zucchini pulp can be used in Zucchini and Olive Frittata (page 143).

serves 4

1. Preheat the oven to 450°F.

2. Cut the zucchini in half lengthwise and scoop out the pulp, reserving it for another use. Salt the inside of the zucchini.

3. Prepare the stuffing by mixing the bread crumbs, currants, pine nuts, onion, parsley, garlic, Pecorino, and black pepper.

4. Lightly oil a baking dish and place the zucchini in it. Fill each zucchini half with stuffing. (The stuffed zucchini can be frozen at this point.) Drizzle olive oil over the stuffing. Layer the mozzarella cheese on top, and spread the tomato sauce on top of the cheese. Bake for 20 minutes. Serve hot.

crispy fried fennel
in light tomato sauce

1 large fennel bulb (about
    2 pounds), trimmed
    and thinly sliced

Flour for dredging

7 tablespoons olive oil

Salt to taste

1 tablespoon tomato
    paste

⅓ cup water

Many people never think of frying fennel, but it is delicious. The edges of the fennel turn crispy golden.

serves 4

1. Blanch the fennel slices in a large pot of boiling salted water for 2 to 3 minutes. Rinse under cold running water and drain well. Dredge the fennel in the flour, shaking off any excess.

2. Heat 6 tablespoons of the olive oil in a large sauté pan over medium-high heat. Sauté the fennel until the edges turn golden, about 3 minutes. Sprinkle with salt, turn the fennel, and continue cooking for 3 to 4 minutes longer.

3. Meanwhile, in a small pot, combine the tomato paste, the remaining 1 tablespoon olive oil, and the cold water and bring to a simmer over medium heat.

4. Pour the tomato sauce over the fennel and cook for 1 minute. Remove from the heat and serve immediately.

Eight

Dolce

For most of us, quick desserts are not as great a priority as a dinner that can be rapidly prepared. Dessert is usually an extra attraction in meal planning for most families, including my own.

When I do want dessert, I often do as the Italians do and opt for my favorite: fruit. Perhaps sliced apples with three Italian cheeses, such as Gorgonzola, Fontina, and Taleggio. Or I might go for some store-bought *panettone,* the Christmas cake made from a yeast dough with raisins and candied fruit, or other bakery treats, such as *struffoli* (crisp honey fritters), any number of the different Italian cookies known as biscotti, the flaky *sfogliatelle,* or, of course, the famous cannoli.

My favorite homemade desserts are fast, light, and healthful fruit desserts. I find a bowl filled with seasonal fresh fruit—peaches, apricots, strawberries, juicy oranges, or apples—perfect after dinner with coffee, espresso, or capuccino. Other times I like to finish with a sweet that is more elaborate, but still quick and easy. The recipes in this chapter are for fruit-based desserts that will satisfy any sweet tooth but can be prepared in no time.

zuppa di frutta esotica

⅓ cup water

2 tablespoons sugar

4 ripe mangoes

2 passion fruit

1 large banana, peeled and sliced

2 kiwis, peeled and sliced

½ teaspoon vanilla extract

Since the days when Venetian merchants first returned from Cairo or the Sea of Azov, Italians have enjoyed the exotic fruits of Africa and the Orient. And today a wide variety of these fruits—mangoes, papayas, plantains, coconuts, kiwis, kumquats, and many more—is available. This dessert soup of tropical fruits is a wonderful summer conclusion to a grilled dish such as Furious Chicken (page 104).

serves 4 to 6

1. In a small saucepan, bring the water to a boil. Add the sugar and stir until it dissolves. Remove from the heat and let cool.

2. Peel and cube the mangoes. The pulp of even ripe mangoes adheres quite rigidly to the pit, so use your hands to squeeze off any pulp you are unable to slice off with a knife. Place the pulp in a large mixing bowl. Cut the passion fruit in half. Pull the seeds, which are edible, and the pulp away from the tough outer skin, and add to the mangoes. Add the banana and kiwis.

3. Stir the vanilla into the cooled sugar syrup, and pour over the fruit. Serve immediately or refrigerate until needed.

bananas in kirsch
and raspberry preserves

2 tablespoons unsalted
   butter

2 bananas, peeled and
   sliced in half
   lengthwise

Confectioner's sugar

6 tablespoons kirsch

6 tablespoons raspberry
   preserves

Ground cinnamon for
   sprinkling

This is delicious, and I love the way the sautéed banana looks, like a sliver of the moon covered with raspberry sauce.

serves 2

1. Melt the butter in a sauté pan. Roll the bananas in confectioner's sugar and add to the pan. Sauté over high heat until the bananas begin to be lightly spotted with brown flecks.

2. Add the kirsch and cook until it has almost evaporated. Add the raspberry preserves, and cook for 2 minutes. Remove to a serving platter, and sprinkle with confectioner's sugar and ground cinnamon. Let cool slightly, and serve.

grilled bananas with peach schnapps

4 bananas (unpeeled)

¼ cup peach schnapps

Confectioner's sugar for
sprinkling

Ground cinnamon for
sprinkling

Grilling bananas is a unique and fun way to prepare them. Make this dish when you can take advantage of a still hot grill from a barbecue dinner.

serves 4

1. Prepare a charcoal fire or preheat a gas grill.

2. Put the unpeeled bananas 1 to 2 inches from the heat source and grill until they blacken on one side, then turn and grill until blackened on both sides.

3. Slice the bananas open lengthwise, leaving them in their skins. Sprinkle 1 tablespoon of the peach schnapps and a shake of confectioner's sugar and cinnamon on each, halve, and serve.

fresh raspberries with mascarpone and rose water

8 ounces mascarpone

½ teaspoon rose water

⅛ teaspoon vanilla
extract

¼ cup sugar

6 ounces raspberries

Because mascarpone is a very rich, creamy cheese, I usually serve this fragrant dessert either long after dinner or mid-afternoon with coffee and store-bought biscotti. Look for rose water in large supermarkets or Middle Eastern markets.

serves 4

1. In a medium bowl, mix together the mascarpone, rose water, vanilla, and sugar until smooth.

2. Place the raspberries in four individual bowls. Put a large dollop of the mascarpone sauce on top of each serving. Serve immediately.

raspberry crespelle

¾ cup flour

2 tablespoons sugar

2 large eggs, beaten

1 cup milk

1 tablespoon unsalted
butter, or more as
needed

¾ cup raspberry
preserves

We follow the French and call them crêpes, but by any name these luscious sweet thin pancakes are my favorite fast dessert. Top them with a sprinkling of confectioner's sugar or cinnamon if desired.

Makes 6 crêpes

1. Put the flour and sugar in a medium bowl. In another bowl, beat the eggs. Add the milk and beat to blend. Pour the egg mixture into the flour, and beat until smooth.

2. In a crêpe pan or small sauté pan, melt 1 tablespoon butter over high heat, coating the bottom of the pan. Pour in a ladleful of batter, quickly turning the pan so the bottom is evenly coated. Cook until golden on the bottom, then, with a spatula, lift the crêpe and flip. Spread 2 tablespoons of the raspberry preserves in the center and fold over the sides. Slide onto a serving plate and keep warm.

3. Continue making crêpes, using more butter as needed. Serve immediately.

poached pears
with coconut whipped cream

1 cup white wine

1 cup orange juice

1 teaspoon brandy

1 cinnamon stick

1 vanilla bean (or
    substitute ⅛
    teaspoon vanilla
    extract)

¼ cup granulated sugar

4 ripe pears

1 cup heavy cream

3 tablespoons
    confectioner's sugar

⅛ teaspoon vanilla
    extract

3 tablespoons sweetened
    coconut flakes, plus
    additional for garnish

Ground cinnamon for
    sprinkling

It looks complicated, but this not-too-sweet poached fruit dessert takes less than half an hour to make.

serves 4

1. In a large pot, combine the white wine, orange juice, brandy, cinnamon stick, vanilla bean (or extract), and granulated sugar, and bring to a boil.

2. Meanwhile, peel the pears. Halve lengthwise and scoop out the cores.

3. Poach the pears in the wine mixture, covered, until tender, about 10 minutes. Remove with a slotted spoon and place in individual serving dishes. Discard the poaching liquid.

4. While the pears are poaching, whip the cream until it forms soft peaks. Fold in the confectioner's sugar, vanilla, and coconut flakes. Refrigerate until needed.

5. Spoon the whipped cream into the hollow of the pears. Sprinkle with coconut flakes and cinnamon, and serve.

peach fritters with cinnamon and honey

Vegetable or corn oil for
deep-frying

1 cup flour

3 tablespoons granulated
sugar

¼ teaspoon salt

2 egg whites, beaten
until frothy

½ to ⅔ cup water

2 ripe peaches, peeled,
pitted, and sliced
into eighths

Orange blossom honey
to taste

Confectioner's sugar for
sprinkling

Ground cinnamon for
sprinkling

In June and July, when peaches are at their peak, I like to treat my family and myself to these special fritters.

serves 4

1. In a large heavy pot or a deep fryer, heat the oil to 360°F.

2. Meanwhile, in a medium bowl, stir together the flour, sugar, and salt. Stir in the egg whites and then ½ cup water. Add more water if the batter is too thick.

3. Dip the peach slices, 4 or 5 at a time, into the batter, letting the excess drip off, and deep-fry just until they turn golden, less than a minute. Move them around as they fry so they don't stick to the pot. With a slotted spoon, remove the fried peaches to paper towels to drain as you cook the rest of the fritters.

4. Place the fritters in individual serving bowls and pour the honey over. Sprinkle with confectioner's sugar and cinnamon, and serve immediately.

peaches with ricotta, pistachio, and apricot sauce

1 large egg, separated

½ cup plus 1 tablespoon sugar

1 tablespoon finely crushed pistachio nuts

1 tablespoon apricot preserves

1 tablespoon finely chopped candied orange peel (see Note)

8 ounces fresh ricotta

1 tablespoon light rum

5 ripe peaches, peeled, halved, and pitted, 1 finely chopped

This rich creamy sauce is perfect in early summer when peaches start coming on the market.

serves 4

1. In the top of a double boiler, combine the egg yolk, 6 tablespoons of the sugar, the pistachios, apricot preserves, candied orange, ricotta, rum, and the chopped peach. Set over simmering water, and whisk constantly until heated. Remove from the heat.

2. In a small bowl, beat the egg white and the remaining 3 tablespoons sugar until the white forms peaks. Fold into the ricotta sauce.

3. Put 2 peach halves in each individual serving bowl, and pour the sauce on top. Serve immediately.

Note: Candied orange peel can be found in supermarkets but I prefer that sold in Middle Eastern markets.

pasta with
honey, sugar, and pistachios

1 cup cooked soup
 pasta, freshly
 cooked and drained
 or reheated until hot

1 tablespoon unsalted
 butter

1 tablespoon honey

¼ cup sugar

¼ teaspoon rose water

1 tablespoon finely
 crushed pistachio
 nuts

This is a unique way to serve "soup" pastas, such as stelline or acini di pepe.

serves 2

1. Combine the hot pasta and all the remaining ingredients and stir to mix. Serve warm or at room temperature.

ricotta and honey

8 ounces ricotta

Orange blossom honey
 to taste

Ground cinnamon for
 sprinkling

An "emergency" dessert for when a sweet tooth strikes, and you are without a cake, tart, or even fruit. This simple recipe will quickly satisfy your yearnings. It's one kids like too.

serves 2 to 4

1. Mix the ricotta cheese and the honey together, or simply drizzle the honey in a decorative pattern over the cheese. Sprinkle cinnamon over, and serve.

Index

Almond(s):
farfalle with artichokes and, 47
fig, and mint cream sauce, veal loin with, 92
meatballs stuffed with mint, mozzarella and, 84
sauce, ziti with lentils, leeks and, 49
spaghetti with broccoli, lemon zest and, 45
Anchovy(ies), 10
and asparagus *panini*, 153
butter, fettuccine with, 27
and capers in white wine, redfish with, 128
and fresh ricotta frittata, 140
Parmesan, and olive *panini*, 153
penne with tomato, basil and, 32
perciatelli with ricotta salata and, 54
red peppers with capers, marjoram and, 171
spaghetti with, 66
spaghetti with red pepper, garlic, parsley and, 26
zucchini with lemon, mint and, 178
Apple, croquettes of veal with walnuts, Taleggio and, 94
Apricot, ricotta, and pistachio sauce, peaches with, 191
Artichoke(s), 10
farfalle with almonds and, 47
frittata, 141
pork with spareribs with sweet and hot peppers and, 98
sauté of sausage, mushrooms and, 100
spaghetti with sausage, mascarpone cream sauce and, 73
tubetti with ricotta, prosciutto, mint, and, 48
Asparagus:
and anchovy *panini*, 153
and crab *panini*, 154

with hot pepper dressing, 175
with pistachios, 176
risotto, 77
Avocado, prosciutto, and tomato *panini*, 150

Baked red snapper with Pantelleria sauce, 126
Baked stuffed zucchini, 180
Baked white fish gratinate, 129
Bananas:
grilled, with peach schnapps, 186
in kirsch and raspberry preserves, 185
Basil, 14
mozzarella, and tomato frittata, 145
penne with tomato, anchovy and, 32
Bass:
grilled fillet of, 121
striped, fettuccine with tomato and, 64
Bay leaves, 14
grilled skewers of sausage, orange and, 99
Bean(s), green:
grilled bluefish, and penne salad, 56
with pine nuts, 162
wrapped in prosciutto, 163
Beef, 84–89
grilled filet mignon with pancetta and rosemary, 89
macaroni salad with grilled steak and vegetables, 39
meatloaf stuffed with eggs, 87
steak pizzaiola, 91
tenderloin with cucumbers and mushrooms, 88
see also Meatballs
Beets, macaroni with mushrooms and, 43
Bel Paese, 12

Bluefish:
    braised in wine and fresh oregano, 125
    grilled, salad of penne, green bean and, 56
    grilled, with oregano, red pepper, and olive
      oil, 124
Boiling, 5
Boston lettuce with herb vinaigrette, 160
Braciola of chicken with mozzarella and herbs,
    109–110
Bread, 10–11
    garlic, 11
Bread crumbs, 11
    spaghetti with oregano, peas and, 40
Breaded shrimp with garlic, lemon zest, and
    parsley, 135
Broccoli:
    with olives and lemon zest, 177
    penne with fennel, endive and, 46
    spaghetti with lemon zest, almonds and, 45
    vermicelli with sardines and, 36
Broiled tomatoes with Fontina, 173
Broken lasagne with portobello mushrooms and
    pancetta, 44
Brussels sprouts, sage rice with sausage and,
    78
Butter, 11
    anchovy, fettuccine with, 27
Butterflied pork tenderloin with nut sauce, 97

Caciocavallo, 12
Capellini with oysters, 57
Capers, 11
    and anchovies in white wine, redfish with,
      128
    do-it-now spaghetti with tuna and, 63
    red peppers with anchovies, marjoram and,
      170
Carrots with Marsala, 161
Cauliflower, sweet-and-sour mushrooms and,
    167
Caviar, salmon, rice with salmon and, 81
Celery:
    roasted red pepper, and olive salad, 158
    sweet-and-sour, 166
Cheese(s), 11–13
    frittata with, 147
    three, perciatelli with two peppers and, 52
    three, tortelloni with, 51
    see also specific cheeses
Chianti, sausage, and pepper stew, quick, 101
Chicken, 104–110
    furious, 104
    with mozzarella and herbs, braciola of, 109–
      110
    with sausage, rosemary, 105
    scallopine with lobster sauce, 108
    spezzatino of peppers, rosemary, wine and,
      106
    spezzatino of squid and, 107

Chicory, spaghetti with dill and, 37
Cinnamon, peach fritters with honey and, 190
Coconut whipped cream, poached pears with,
    189
Cooking methods, 3–5
Crab and asparagus panini, 154
Cream, 13
Cream sauce:
    fig, almond, and mint, veal loin with, 92
    garlic, shrimp in, 136
    sausage and artichoke mascarpone, spaghetti
      with, 73
Crispy fried fennel in light tomato sauce, 181
Croquettes:
    swordfish, in tomato sauce, 116–117
    of veal with apple, walnuts, and Taleggio, 94
Cucina rapida:
    cooking methods for, 3–5
    general information for, 1–7
    ingredients for, 10–20
    roots of, 2
    tips for, 6
Cucumbers, beef tenderloin with mushrooms
    and, 88
Currants, 13

Deep-frying, 4–5
Desserts, 183–191
    poached pears with coconut whipped cream,
      189
    ricotta and honey, 192
    zuppa di frutta esotica, 184
    see also Bananas; Peach(es); Raspberry(ies)
Dill, spaghetti with chicory and, 37
Do-it-now spaghetti with tuna and capers, 63
Duck with tangerine sauce, 113–114

Egg(s):
    with fish roe, 148
    fried, perciatelli with, 28
    meatloaf stuffed with, 87
    sliced, and shrimp panini, 152
    see also Frittatas
Endive, penne with broccoli, fennel and, 46
Equipment, 6

Farfalle with almonds and artichokes, 47
Fennel:
    in light tomato sauce, crispy fried, 181
    onion, tomato, and green olive salad, 159
    penne with broccoli, endive and, 46
Fennel seed, 15
Fettuccine:
    with anchovy butter, 27
    with Fontina fondue, 50
    with mint, walnut, and mascarpone pesto, 55
    with prosciutto and zucchini blossoms, 67
    with salsa a crudo, 34

with striped bass and tomato, 64
with veal marrow and ricotta, 69
Fig(s):
    almond, and mint cream sauce, veal loin
        with, 92
    prosciutto, and mozzarella *panini*, fresh, 154
    tomato stuffed with prosciutto, mint and, 170
Filet mignon with pancetta and rosemary,
        grilled, 89
Fish, 13–14, 115–130
    monkfish nuggets, 130
    parsley-stuffed grilled porgy and mackerel,
        123
    redfish with capers and anchovies in white
        wine, 128
    sardines gratinate, 137
    white, baked gratinate of, 129
    see also Bass; Bluefish; Red snapper;
        Salmon; Shellfish; Swordfish
Fish roe, eggs with, 148
Fontina, 12
    broiled tomatoes with, 173
    fondue, fettuccine with, 50
    turkey scallopine with sage, olives, tomato
        and, 111
    and ziti frittata, 142
Food processors, 5
Fowl, 83, 104–114
    duck with tangerine sauce, 113–114
    see also Chicken; Turkey
Fresh fig, prosciutto, and mozzarella *panini*,
        154
Fresh raspberries with mascarpone and rose
        water, 187
Fresh ricotta and anchovy frittata, 140
Fried meatballs, 85
Frittatas, 139–149
    artichoke, 141
    con formaggio, 147
    fresh ricotta and anchovy, 140
    Gorgonzola, olive, and tomato, 144
    mozzarella, tomato, and basil, 145
    pancetta and Parmesan, 146
    pizza, 149
    ziti and Fontina, 142
    zucchini and olive, 143
Fritters:
    peach, with cinnamon and honey, 90
    turkey breast, 112
Furious chicken, 104
Fusilli:
    with pork and sweet pepper, 68
    with vegetables and herbs, 42

Garlic, 14
    bread, 11
    breaded shrimp with lemon zest, parsley
        and, 135
    cream sauce, shrimp in, 136

herbed, spaghetti with tomato, shrimp and,
        61
    and parsley shrimp, 134
    salmon with tomato, mint and, 122
    spaghetti with red pepper, anchovies, parsley
        and, 26
    spinach sautéed in olive oil and, 164
    zucchini with oregano and, 179
Gobbets of pork with sweet pepper, 96
Gorgonzola, 12
    olive, and tomato frittata, 144
Grilled bananas with peach schnapps, 186
Grilled bluefish, penne, and green bean salad,
        56
Grilled bluefish with oregano, red pepper, and
        olive oil, 124
Grilled filet mignon with pancetta and
        rosemary, 89
Grilled fillet of bass, 121
Grilled red snapper *alla calabrese*, 127
Grilled skewers of sausage, orange, and bay
        leaf, 99
Grilled swordfish with orange and thyme, 118
Grilled swordfish with *sammurigghiu* sauce, 119
Grilling, 3–4

Hazelnuts, veal with, 93
Hearts of palm and prosciutto *panini*, 151
Herb(s) and spices, 14–15
    braciola of chicken with mozzarella and, 109–
        110
    fusilli with vegetables and, 42
    rigatoni with olives and, 31
    vinaigrette, Boston lettuce with, 160
    see also specific herbs and spices
Honey, 15
    pasta with sugar, pistachios and, 192
    peach fritters with cinnamon and, 190
    ricotta and, 192

Ingredients, 10–20

Kidney(s):
    with fried onions, rosemary, and sage, 103
    penne with zucchini and, 71
Kirsch, bananas in raspberry preserves and, 185

Lamb kidneys with fried onions, rosemary, and
        sage, 103
Lamb with pancetta, mint, and orange zest, 95
Lasagne, broken, with portobello mushrooms
        and pancetta, 44
Leeks, ziti with lentils, almond sauce and, 49
Leftovers, 2–3
Lemon:
    linguine with shrimp, spinach and, 58–59
    zucchini with anchovies, mint and, 178

Lemon zest:
    breaded shrimp with garlic, parsley and, 135
    broccoli with olives and, 177
Lentils, ziti with leeks, almond sauce and, 49
Lettuce, Boston, with herb vinaigrette, 160
Linguine:
    with crushed black pepper, 25
    with shrimp, spinach, and lemon, 58–59
    with spicy shrimp and peppers, 60
Liqueur, 15
Liver, perciatelli with pistachios, green
    peppercorns and, 70
Lobster:
    sauce, chicken scallopine with, 108
    spaghetti with hot chili peppers and, 62

Macaroni:
    with beets and mushrooms, 43
    con le verdure, 38
    leftover, pizzaiola sauce for, 29
    salad with grilled steak and vegetables, 39
Mackerel, parsley-stuffed grilled porgy and, 123
Marjoram, 15
    red peppers with capers, anchovies and, 171
Marsala:
    carrots with, 161
    sauce, sage meatballs with, 86
Mascarpone, 12
    fresh raspberries with rose water, 187
    mint, and walnut pesto, fettuccine with, 55
    sausage, and artichoke cream sauce,
        spaghetti with, 73
Meat, 83–103
    lamb with pancetta, mint, and orange zest,
        95
    see also Beef; Pork; Veal
Meatballs:
    fried, 85
    sage, with Marsala sauce, 86
    stuffed with almonds, mint, and mozzarella,
        84
Meatloaf stuffed with eggs, 87
Microwaving, 5
Mint, 15
    fig, and almond cream sauce, veal loin with,
        92
    lamb with pancetta, orange zest and, 95
    meatballs stuffed with almonds, mozzarella
        and, 84
    rice and parsley and, 76
    salmon with tomato, garlic and, 122
    spaghetti with sardine, tomato and, 35
    sweet-and-sour squash with, 168
    tomato stuffed with prosciutto, figs and, 170
    tubetti with ricotta, artichokes, prosciutto
        and, 48
    walnut and mascarpone pesto, fettuccine
        with, 55
    zucchini with anchovies, lemon and, 178

Mixed vegetable sauté, 169
Monkfish nuggets, 130
Mozzarella, 12
    braciola of chicken with herbs and, 109–110
    in *carrozza*, 155
    fresh fig, and prosciutto *panini*, 154
    meatballs stuffed with almonds, mint and, 84
    and olive *panini*, 152
    and porchetta *panino*, 150
    roasted red peppers stuffed with prosciutto
        and, 174
    tomato, and basil frittata, 145
Mushrooms, 15–16
    beef tenderloin with cucumbers and, 88
    macaroni with beets and, 43
    portobello, broken lasagne with pancetta and,
        44
    sauté of sausage, artichokes and, 100
    sweet-and-sour cauliflower and, 167
Mussel(s):
    steamed, 132–133
    and tomato salad, 131

Nut(s), 16
    sauce, butterflied pork tenderloin with, 97
    see also Almond(s); Pine nuts; Pistachio(s);
        Walnut(s)

Olive oil, 16–17
    grilled bluefish with oregano, red pepper
        and, 124
    spaghetti with parsley, red chili pepper and,
        24
    spinach sautéed in garlic and, 164
Olive(s), 17
    black, penne with yellow pepper, tomatoes
        and, 33
    broccoli with lemon zest and, 177
    celery, and roasted red pepper salad, 158
    Gorgonzola, and tomato frittata, 144
    green, fennel, onion, and tomato salad, 159
    and mozzarella *panini*, 152
    Parmesan, and anchovy *panini*, 153
    rigatoni with herbs and, 31
    turkey scallopine with sage, tomato, Fontina
        and, 111
    and zucchini frittata, 143
Onion(s):
    fennel, tomato, and green olive salad, 159
    fried, kidneys with rosemary, sage and, 103
Orange:
    grilled skewers of sausage, bay leaf and, 99
    grilled swordfish with thyme and, 118
Orange zest, lamb with pancetta, mint and, 95
Oregano, 15
    fresh, bluefish braised in wine and, 125
    grilled bluefish with red pepper, olive oil
        and, 124

oven-roasted tomatoes with provolone, pine
    nuts and, 172
spaghetti with bread crumbs, peas and, 40
zucchini with garlic and, 179
Oven-roasted tomatoes with provolone, pine
    nuts, and oregano, 172
Oysters:
    capellini with, 57
    sesame fried, 133

Pancetta, 17
    broken lasagne with portobello mushrooms
        and, 44
    grilled filet mignon with rosemary and, 89
    lamb with mint, orange zest and, 95
    and Parmesan frittata, 146
Panini, 139, 149–154
    asparagus and anchovy, 153
    crab and asparagus, 154
    fresh fig, prosciutto, and mozzarella, 154
    olives and mozzarella, 152
    Parmesan, olive, and anchovy, 153
    porchetta and mozzarella, 150
    prosciutto, avocado, and tomato, 150
    prosciutto and hearts of palm, 151
    Taleggio and tomato, 151
Pantelleria sauce, baked red snapper with, 126
Parmesan (Parmigiano-Reggiano), 12–13
    olive, and anchovy *panini*, 153
    and pancetta frittata, 146
    spaghetti with ricotta, white wine and, 53
Parsley, 15
    breaded shrimp with garlic, lemon zest and,
        135
    and garlic shrimp, 134
    -stuffed grilled porgy and mackerel, 123
Pasta, 23–73
    broken lasagne with portobello mushrooms
        and pancetta, 44
    capellini with oysters, 57
    farfalle with almonds and artichokes, 47
    general information about, 17–18
    with honey, sugar, and pistachios, 192
    rigatoni with olives and herbs, 31
    tortelloni with three cheeses, 51
    vermicelli with broccoli and sardines, 37
    ziti with lentils, leeks, and almond sauce, 49
    see also Fettuccine; Fusilli; Linguine;
        Macaroni; Penne; Perciatelli; Spaghetti;
        Tubetti
Peach(es):
    fritters with cinnamon and honey, 191
    with ricotta, pistachio, and apricot sauce, 190
    schnapps, grilled bananas with, 186
Pears, poached, with coconut whipped cream,
    189
Peas, 18
    spaghetti with oregano, bread crumbs and,
        40

tubetti with prosciutto and, 41
Pecorino, 13
Penne:
    with broccoli, fennel and endive, 46
    grilled bluefish, and green bean salad, 56
    with kidney and zucchini, 71
    with tomato, basil, and anchovy, 32
    with yellow pepper, black olives, and
        tomatoes, 33
Peperoncini, 18
Pepper, black (peppercorns), 14, 15
    crushed, linguine with, 25
Pepper, yellow bell, penne with black olives,
    tomatoes and, 33
Peppercorns, green, perciatelli with liver,
    pistachios and, 70
Peppers:
    linguine with spicy shrimp and, 60
    spezzatino of veal with tomatoes and, 90
Pepper(s), red bell, 19
    with capers, anchovies, and marjoram, 171
    roasted, celery and olive salad with, 158
    roasted, stuffed with mozzarella and
        prosciutto, 174
Pepper(s), red chili, 19
    dressing, asparagus with, 175
    grilled bluefish with oregano, olive oil and, 124
    pork spareribs with artichokes and sweet
        peppers and, 98
    spaghetti with garlic, anchovies, parsley and,
        26
    spaghetti with lobster and, 62
    spaghetti with olive oil, parsley and, 24
Pepper(s), sweet:
    fusilli with pork and, 68
    gobbets of pork with, 96
    pork spareribs with artichokes and hot
        peppers and, 98
    sausage, and Chianti stew, quick, 101
    spezzatino of chicken with rosemary, wine
        and, 106
Perciatelli:
    with fried eggs, 28
    with liver, pistachios, and green peppercorns,
        70
    with ricotta salata and anchovies, 54
    with three cheeses and two peppers, 52
Pesto, mint, walnut, and mascarpone, fettuccine
    with, 55
Pine nuts:
    green beans with, 162
    oven-roasted tomatoes with provolone,
        oregano and, 172
Pistachio(s):
    asparagus with, 176
    pasta with honey, sugar and, 192
    perciatelli with liver, green peppercorns and,
        70
    ricotta, and apricot sauce, peaches with, 191

Pizza, frittata, 149
Pizzaiola sauce:
   for leftover macaroni, 29
   steak with, 91
Poached pears with coconut whipped cream, 189
Porchetta, 18
Porchetta and mozzarella *panino*, 150
Porgy, parsley-stuffed grilled mackerel and, 123
Pork, 96–102
   fusilli with sweet pepper and, 68
   spareribs with artichokes and sweet and hot peppers, 98
   with sweet pepper, gobbets of, 96
   tenderloin with nut sauce, butterflied, 97
   see also Pancetta; Prosciutto; Sausage
Prosciutto, 18–19
   avocado, and tomato *panini*, 150
   fettuccine with zucchini blossoms and, 67
   fresh fig, and mozzarella *panini*, 154
   green beans wrapped in, 163
   and hearts of palm *panini*, 151
   roasted red peppers stuffed with mozzarella and, 174
   tomato stuffed with figs, mint and, 170
   tubetti with peas and, 41
   tubetti with ricotta, artichokes, mint and, 48
Provolone, 13
   oven-roasted tomatoes with pine nuts, oregano and, 172

Quick sausage, pepper, and Chianti stew, 101

Raisins, 19
Raspberry(ies):
   crespelle, 188
   fresh, with mascarpone and rose water, 187
   preserves, bananas in kirsch and, 185
Recipes:
   note on, 21
   reading of, 6
Redfish, with capers and anchovies in white wine, 128
Red peppers with capers, anchovies, and marjoram, 171
Red snapper:
   baked, with Pantelleria sauce, 126
   grilled, *alla calabrese*, 127
Rice, 19, 75–81
   with Brussels sprouts and sausage, sage, 78
   with parsley and mint, 76
   saffron, *alla marinara*, 80
   with saffron shrimp, 79
   with salmon and salmon caviar, 81
Ricotta, 13
   and anchovy frittata, 140
   fettuccine with veal marrow and, 69
   and honey, 192

pistachio, and apricot sauce, peaches with, 191
spaghetti with Parmesan, white wine and, 53
tubetti with artichokes, prosciutto, mint and, 48
Ricotta salata, 13
   perciatelli with anchovies and, 54
Rigatoni with olives and herbs, 31
Risotto, asparagus, 77
Roasted red peppers stuffed with mozzarella and prosciutto, 174
Rosemary, 15
   chicken with sausage, 105
   grilled filet mignon with pancetta and, 89
   kidneys with fried onions, sage and, 103
   spezzatino of chicken with peppers, wine and, 106
   tomato, and sausage sauce, spaghetti with, 72
Rose water, fresh raspberries with mascarpone and, 187

Saffron, 15
   rice *alla marinara*, 80
   shrimp, rice with, 79
Sage, 15
   kidneys with fried onions, rosemary and, 103
   meatballs with Marsala sauce, 86
   rice with Brussels sprouts and sausage, 78
   turkey scallopine with olives, tomato, Fontina and, 111
Salad(s):
   celery, roasted red pepper, and olive, 158
   fennel, onion, tomato, and green olive, 159
   mussel and tomato, 131
Salad(s), pasta:
   macaroni, grilled steak, and vegetables, 39
   penne, grilled bluefish, and green bean, 56
Salmon:
   rice with salmon caviar and, 81
   with tomato, mint, and garlic, 122
Salsa a crudo, fettuccine with, 34
Salt, 15
Sardine(s), 19
   gratinate, 137
   spaghetti with tomato, mint and, 35
   vermicelli with broccoli and, 36
Sauce(s):
   almond, ziti with lentils, leeks and, 49
   lobster, chicken scallopine with, 108
   Marsala, sage meatballs with, 86
   nut, butterflied pork tenderloin with, 97
   Pantelleria, baked red snapper with, 126
   pizzaiola, for leftover macaroni, 29
   pizzaiola, steak with, 91
   ricotta, pistachio, and apricot, peaches with, 191
   sammurigghiu, grilled swordfish with, 119

tangerine, duck with, 113–114
see also Cream sauce; Tomato sauce
Sausage, 19
  and artichoke mascarpone cream sauce,
    spaghetti with, 73
  orange, and bay leaf, grilled skewers of, 99
  pepper, and Chianti stew, quick, 101
  rosemary chicken with, 105
  sage rice with Brussels sprouts and, 78
  sauté of mushrooms, artichokes and, 100
  in sweet-and-sour tomato sauce, 102
  tomato, and rosemary sauce, spaghetti with,
    72
Sautéed red Swiss chard, 165
Sautéing, 3
Sauté of sausage, mushrooms and artichokes,
  100
Savory, 15
Scallops, spaghetti with swordfish and, 65
Sesame fried oysters, 133
Shellfish, 131–136
  crab and asparagus *panini*, 154
  see also Lobster; Mussel(s); Oysters; Shrimp
Shrimp:
  breaded, with garlic lemon zest, and parsley,
    135
  garlic and parsley, 134
  in garlic cream sauce, 136
  linguine with spinach, lemon and,
    58–59
  saffron, rice with, 79
  and sliced egg *panini*, 152
  spicy, linguine with peppers and, 60
  tomato, spaghetti with herbed garlic and, 61
Soffritto, 19
Spaghetti:
  with anchovies, 66
  with broccoli, lemon zest, and almonds, 45
  with chicory and dill, 37
  with fried zucchini, 30
  with herbed garlic and tomato shrimp, 61
  with lobster and hot chili peppers, 62
  with olive oil, parsley, and red chili pepper,
    24
  with oregano, bread crumbs and peas, 40
  with Parmesan, ricotta, and white wine, 53
  with red pepper, garlic, anchovies, and
    parsley, 26
  with sardine, tomato, and mint, 35
  with sausage and artichoke mascarpone
    cream sauce, 73
  with swordfish and scallops, 65
  with tomato, sausage, and rosemary sauce,
    72
  with tuna and capers, do-it-now, 63
Spezzatino:
  of chicken and squid, 107
  of chicken with peppers, rosemary, and wine,
    106

of veal with peppers and tomatoes, 90
Spices and herbs, *see* Herb(s) and spices
Spinach:
  linguine with shrimp, lemon and, 58–59
  sautéed in garlic and olive oil, 164
Squash with mint, sweet-and-sour, 168
Squid, 19–20
  spezzatino of chicken and, 107
Steak:
  grilled, macaroni salad with vegetables and,
    39
  grilled filet mignon with pancetta and
    rosemary, 89
  pizzaiola, 91
Steamed mussels, 132–133
Stew:
  quick sausage, pepper, and Chianti, 101
  see also Spezzatino
Stock, 20
Sweet-and-sour cauliflower and mushrooms, 167
  167
Sweet-and-sour celery, 166
Sweet-and-sour squash with mint, 168
Sweet-and-sour tomato sauce, sausage in, 102
Swiss chard, sautéed red, 165
Swordfish, 116–120
  croquettes in tomato sauce, 116–117
  grilled, with orange and thyme, 118
  grilled, with *sammurigghiu* sauce, 119
  pizzaiola, 120
  spaghetti with scallops and, 65

Taleggio, 13
  croquettes of veal with apple, walnuts and,
    94
  and tomato *panini*, 151
Tangerine sauce, duck with, 113–114
Thyme, 15
  grilled swordfish with orange and, 118
Timesaving techniques, 7
Tomato(es), 20
  fennel, onion, and green olive salad, 159
  fettuccine with striped bass and, 64
  with Fontina, broiled, 173
  Gorgonzola, and olive frittata, 144
  mozzarella, and basil frittata, 146
  and mussel salad, 131
  oven-roasted, with provolone, pine nuts, and
    oregano, 172
  penne with basil, anchovy and, 32
  penne with yellow pepper, black olives and,
    33
  prosciutto, and avocado *panini*, 150
  salmon with mint, garlic and, 122
  shrimp, spaghetti with herbed garlic and, 61
  spaghetti with sardine, mint and, 35
  spezzatino of veal with peppers and, 90
  stuffed with prosciutto, figs, and mint, 170
  and Taleggio *panini*, 151

Tomato(es) *(cont.)*
  turkey scallopine with sage, olives, Fontina
    and, 111
Tomato sauce:
  light, crispy fried fennel in, 181
  spaghetti with sausage, rosemary and, 72
  sweet-and-sour, sausage in, 102
  swordfish croquettes in, 116–117
Tortelloni with three cheeses, 51
Tubetti:
  with peas and prosciutto, 41
  with ricotta, artichokes, prosciutto, and mint,
    48
Tuna, 20
  do-it-now spaghetti with capers and, 63
Turkey:
  breast fritters, 112
  scallopine with sage, olives, tomato, and
    Fontina, 111

Veal, 92–94
  with apple, walnuts, and Taleggio, croquettes
    of, 94
  with hazelnuts, 93
  loin with fig, almond, and mint cream sauce,
    92
  spezzatino of peppers, tomatoes and, 90
Veal marrow, fettuccine with ricotta and, 69
Vegetables and side dishes, 157–181
  fusilli with herbs and, 42
  macaroni con le verdure, 38
  macaroni salad with grilled steak and, 39
  sauté, mixed, 169
  see also specific vegetables
Vermicelli with broccoli and sardines, 36

Vinaigrette, herb, Boston lettuce with, 160
Vinegar, 20

Walnut(s):
  croquettes of veal with apple, Taleggio and,
    94
  mint, and mascarpone pesto, fettuccine with,
    55
White fish gratinate, baked, 129
Wine, 20
  quick sausage, pepper, and Chianti stew, 101
  spezzatino of chicken with peppers, rosemary
    and, 106
  white, bluefish braised in fresh oregano and,
    125
  white, redfish with capers and anchovies in,
    128
  white, spaghetti with Parmesan, ricotta and,
    53
  see also Marsala

Ziti:
  and Fontina frittata, 142
  with lentils, leeks, and almond sauce, 49
Zucchini:
  with anchovies, lemon, and mint, 178
  baked stuffed, 180
  fried, spaghetti with, 30
  and olive frittata, 143
  with oregano and garlic, 179
  penne with kidney and, 71
Zucchini blossoms, fettuccine with prosciutto
    and, 67
Zuppa di frutta esotica, 184